Radical Utu

Ohio University Research in International Studies

This series of publications on Africa, Latin America, Southeast Asia, and Global and Comparative Studies is designed to present significant research, translation, and opinion to area specialists and to a wide community of persons interested in world affairs. The series is distributed worldwide. For more information, consult the Ohio University Press website, ohioswallow.com.

Books in the Ohio University Research in International Studies series are published by Ohio University Press in association with the Center for International Studies. The views expressed in individual volumes are those of the authors and should not be considered to represent the policies or beliefs of the Center for International Studies, Ohio University Press, or Ohio University.

Radical Utu

CRITICAL IDEAS
AND IDEALS OF
WANGARI MUTA MAATHAI

Besi Brillian Muhonja

Ohio University Research in International Studies
Africa Series No. 95
Ohio University Press
Athens

Ohio University Press, Athens, Ohio 45701
ohioswallow.com
© 2020 by Ohio University Press

To obtain permission to quote, reprint, or otherwise reproduce or distribute
material from
Ohio University Press publications, please contact our rights and permissions
department at
(740) 593-1154 or (740) 593-4536 (fax).

Printed in the United States of America
The books in the Ohio University Research in International Studies Series
are printed on acid-free paper ⊚ ™

30 29 28 27 26 25 24 23 22 21 20   5 4 3 2 1

Library of Congress Cataloging-in-Publication Data

Names: Muhonja, Besi Brillian, author.
Title: Radical utu : critical ideas and ideals of Wangari Muta Maathai /
Besi Brillian Muhonja.
Description: Athens, Ohio : Ohio University Press, 2020. | Series: Ohio
University Research in International Studies, Africa Series | Includes
bibliographical references and index.
Identifiers: LCCN 2020002544 | ISBN 9780896803268 (paperback) | ISBN
9780896805071 (pdf)
Subjects: LCSH: Maathai, Wangari. | Women intellectuals--Kenya. | Women
conservationists--Kenya. | Women political activists--Kenya. |
Kenya—Intellectual life. | Kenya--Politics and government. |
Decolonization--Kenya. | Philosophy, African.
Classification: LCC DT433.582.M24 M84 2020 | DDC 967.6204092--dc23
LC record available at https://lccn.loc.gov/2020002544

Dedicated to

Vaa Muhonja

Contents

Preface

Literature available on Professor Wangari Muta Maathai primarily focuses on her work with the Green Belt Movement and the 2004 conferment of the Nobel Peace Prize. In most accounts, the scholar and critical thinker are lost in celebrations of the activist, and the activist is very narrowly feted. This book focuses on Maathai's thoughts, words, and works, locating them in the global map of knowledge production, an exercise necessary to the project of centering African thinkers in the academy and in scholarship in general.[1] With a larger-than-life profile like Maathai's, it is easy for the person and public history to overshadow engagement with the ideas. For this reason, I invite readers to privilege, in their encounter with this text, the analysis, philosophies, and theories presented.

The philosophical and theoretical legacies of Maathai's at times controversy-inspiring life and work have not, until now, been examined in a book-length monograph. Engaging her as a scholar-activist, this interdisciplinary undertaking goes beyond the simple recording of herstory to tease out her world senses and critical thinking on four main subjects: women's empowerment and liberation, environmentalism, democratic spaces, and globalization and global governance. Writing this book involved years of mining and reviewing publications, speeches, interviews, and news reports by and on Maathai and identifying recurring subjects. I consolidated and analyzed the material, and for each topical area I isolated clusters of themes, which provided directions for framing solid concepts. In order to articulate and engage them, it was necessary to christen some concepts, philosophies, and theories. I endeavored to maintain the integrity of Maathai's thoughts and words in the processes of functionalizing and naming these ideas and locating them in dialogue with each other.

The book is quote-heavy to authentically represent Maathai's ideas and allow the reader access to not just the meaning but also the spirit of her words and voice. Through this direct encounter with her words, readers may trace the development of Maathai's thoughts and identify fresh associations, concepts, contexts, and frameworks to further the work this book begins. My purpose is to present her ideas and ideals in a way that scholars, activists, and policymakers can study, apply, test, question, critique, or even challenge in their own work. It is not my intent to register Maathai as the absolute originator of all the thoughts isolated during this sojourn into her world. Rather, I outline how the application of her unique lens prompts new practical and epistemological implications for those ideas. Emerging from this exertion a principal philosophy and lens through which I conceive the arguments of the book and which I name "radical *utu*."

Exploring Maathai's world and world senses, I delineate radical utu as a driving idea and ideal. In a nod to her promotion of indigenous African ways of knowing and languages (Maathai 1995a, 2009b), I use the Swahili word *utu* to reference what Maathai signified as "what it means to be human." This orients radical living as both a philosophy and an active process—individuals and communities (re) imagining themselves as engaged in relations and encounters with other humans rooted in ethics and values of equity and honor for the humanity of others and for their environments.

Actuating utu is an exercise in expediting humanness and humanity. Utu, under different appellations, is a philosophy and principle that undergirds the community organization of many indigenous African societies. *Utu* is the Swahili word for *ubuntu*. That concept is a reality in many African cultures and languages, even in non-Bantu areas—for example, *nitey* among the Wolof in Senegal and The Gambia. The Bantu word has phonological variants across communities, including *bumonto* in Kichiga/Kiganda (Uganda), *bumuntu* in Kisukuma and Kihaya (Tanzania), *vumuntu* in Shitsonga and Shitswa (Mozambique), *bomoto* in Bobangi (Democratic Republic of Congo), *ubumuntu* in Kinyarwanda, and *gimuntu* in Gikongo and Gikwese (DRC, Angola). The term *utu* is appropriate for this application because it typifies multiple significations. *Utu* allows us to mediate that colossal inquiry proffered by Maathai—what it means to be human (Maathai 2010a, 16–17)—from a number of perspectives. The noun for "person" in the Swahili language is *mtu*. *Utu* therefore, first and foremost, simply indicates the reality of being a person as opposed to another entity. This designation of *utu* has as its closest English equivalent the phrase "being a human being." *Utu* denotes person-hood. *Utu* may also be used to identify one's unique personality that is grounded by the fact that one has personhood—a performance of personhood, so to speak. Another interpretation of *utu* is "human-ness"—the capacity to "do" being human through exhibiting what would be considered human qualities such as conscience, ethics, emotion, considerate sense, and spirituality. These makings of utu, signifying desirable human nature, are supposed to set human beings apart from other occupiers of our universe (17). As Maathai noted, "They define our humanity" (16). Utu, therefore, also speaks to the common essentiality of humans. She elaborated on the universality of this character of utu, saying, "These values are not contained only within certain religions, neither does one have to profess a faith in a divine being to live by them. However, they do seem to be a part of human nature, and I'm convinced that we are better people because we hold them, and that humankind is better off with them, than without them" (16).

Four chapters of this book, analyzing the identified topical areas through the lens of radical utu, are sandwiched between two chapters that locate Maathai in history. There is a rationale behind this organization. Chapter 1 offers an introduction to cleanse the previously identified limited characterization of Wangari Muta Maathai in the minds of some readers before they engage with her ideas. The chapter also familiarizes those who have not yet encountered Maathai with her life and works. Unlike the rest of the chapters, which combine critical analysis and narrative forms, this chapter employs a predominantly narrative voice to meet the second goal of its inclusion—allowing readers to encounter the person in order to appreciate the making of the critical thinker. Because she did not see the different facets of her life, scholarship, and activism as independent from each other, I present her different roles, practices, and identities as additive, constituting the aggregative creation of the person in history: family member *and* scholar *and* public leader *and* activist *and* politician.

In the final chapter, I raise the question of legacy and examine the extent to which Maathai's ideas and ideals have been preserved or propagated in scholarship and activism. Within that investigation, Maathai's narrative provides a platform that allows me to engage the subject of the historical erasure of critical African thinkers in scholarship, the academy, and beyond. It is my hope that this presentation of Maathai as a thought influencer advances the goals of initiatives responding to this urgent challenge.

Acknowledgments

I am indebted to family members, mentors, collaborators, and friends. Vaa Muhonja, Mama, Mideva, Kegehi, Kisia, and Buyanzi, and our children, Yvonne, Ivy, Shani, Adisa, J, Taye, Ella, Amy, and Kay—you continue to inspire and motivate me. I love you. I am grateful to my mentors, Nkiru Nzegwu, Joanne Gabbin, David Owusu-Ansah, Don Boros, and Lamont King, and to my sister, Taimi Castle, and brothers, Khadim Thiam and Evan Mwangi, whose personal and academic insights feed my work and life. I wish to especially recognize Nkiru Nzegwu, who in 2005, sharing my respect for Wangari Maathai, helped direct my admiration of her into academic curiosity. I am grateful for the partnerships I enjoy with the academic and professional staff and students at the Wangari Maathai Institute for Peace and Environmental Studies.

Asanteni sana for emotional, intellectual, and other support to dear friends Peter Ng'ang'a, Ndirangu wa Maina, Ian Mbugua, Angela Rarieya, Gillianne Obaso, Imali "Octi" Onyango, Brian Kiai, Musa Nyandusi, Babacar Mbaye, Marame Gueye, Oyunga Pala, Quito Swan, Betty Wambui, Mollie Godfrey, Lauren Alleyne, Sofia Samatar, Case Watkins, Chris Blake, Heather Coltman, Bill Van Norman, Neil Marrin, Melissa Lubin, Mary O'Donnell, Marina Shafik, Chris Arndt, Ann-Janine Morey, Kristen Wylie, Aderonke Adesanya, Adebayo Ogundipe, Jane Mutune Mutheu, Shadrack Nasong'o, Olufemi Taiwo, Kwame Edwin Otu, Achola Pala, Mshai Mwangola, Kithaka wa Mberia, Tushabe wa Tushabe, Lilian Passos Wichert Feitosa, Gianluca De Fazio, Heather Scheuerman, Chase Martin, Tara Kristiansen, Lars Kristiansen, Benjamin Meade, Terry Beitzel, and Robert Goebel. To interlocutors Stephen I. Ng'ang'a, Stephen Gitahi Kiama, Nzioka J. Muthama, and my Harrisonburg family—thank you. I am thankful to my colleagues and students at James Madison University, who shared the development and explorations of parts of this book with me. Appreciation goes out especially to the Sisters in Session collective, Robert Aguirre, Chris Arndt, Dabney Bankert, Brian Flota, Rose Gray, Angela Carter, Amanda Roadcap, and the Africana Literatures and Cultures Workshop crew. Maureen Kegehi and Rony Wesonga, thank you for helping manage my logistics for research and writing. I recognize the value of the financial support toward the production of this work from the Carnegie African Diaspora Fellowship Program and the following sources and units at James Madison University: Provost's Summer Research Grant, College of Arts and Letters Dean's International Travel Grant, the Office of Access and Inclusion, the Department of English, and the Center for Global Engagement. Lillie Jacobs and Michelle Pineda-Hernandez, I could not have asked for better research assistants.

Keith Miller, thank you for your skill. Gill Berchowitz, Ricky Huard, and the rest of the Ohio University Press team, working with you has been an absolute pleasure.

1

Birthing Radical Selves

The Making of a Scholar-Activist

This chapter chronicles Wangari Muta Maathai's experiential history with the topics engaged in the rest of the book—environmental management and justice, critical feminisms, democratic spaces, and globalization and global governance systems. It is my hope that the reader will gain a degree of appreciation for the events and journeys that molded Maathai and shaped her politics and critical thinking. Through the seasons of her life, I recount the advent of her activist and scholarly identities, selves, and roles. I draw her narrative primarily from her memoir, interviews, and media reports and meld it with Kenyan and global histories of the different seasons of her scholarship and activism.

Wangari Muta was born on April 1, 1940, in the village of Ihithe, Nyeri, in the central highlands of what was then British Kenya, to peasant farmers Muta Njugi and Wanjiru Muta, who were members of the Gikuyu ethnic group (Maathai 2007a, 3–4). She was the third of six children and the first daughter of her biological mother. Her earliest memories on record are mostly connected to experiences with her mother, with whom she was very close. Growing up in a polygamous family, she remembered the four mothers living mostly in harmony and being supportive of each other, although she acknowledged the existence of some dissonance in the family and that her father beat his wives (19). Nevertheless, she reflected on her childhood with unmistakable nostalgia. Her earliest memories place her family residing and working on a farm in Nakuru belonging to a settler named Mr. Neyland (14–28). In 1947, Wangari, her mother, and her sisters left the farm to join her brothers on the family's ancestral land in Ihithe. This move increased young Wangari's responsibilities as eldest daughter within the home and family (37). She said, "I was very much my mother's helper . . . literally almost emulating her and being a little woman around the house" (2009a).

Historical, political, and social coincidences stimulated the early development of what would become Maathai's distinctive personality—as a radical humanist and defender of women's and human rights and the environment—and grounded what would become her value system, *utu*. Her childhood was punctuated by significant moments in Kenya's political history. The early years of her life coincided with the founding of nationalist initiatives and movements by African Kenyans. At the time, Jomo Kenyatta had become leader of the Kenya African Union (KAU), formerly the Kenya African Study Union, amid rumblings of nationalism. Adding to the development of her person was her family's appreciation for formal education. Members of her extended family were part of the *athomi*, translating to "readers" or "those who could read." This was the moniker assigned to those who had acquired some level of formal education, a status distinction that abetted the construction of social classes during and after colonialism. Wangari started her formal education at Ihithe Primary School, following the intervention of her brother, Nderitu, and her mother's agreement to send the young girl to school (Maathai 2007a, 39). Here began her journey as *muthomi*, a reader, a scholar. Thus, the muthomi was born in an environment that also supported the genesis of her political and environmental consciousness. At the same time, Wangari started her life as a farmer, a lover of the environment.

Wangari tended year-round a small plot of land given to her by her mother, even while she helped her mother and brothers cultivate the larger family land (Maathai 2007a, 46). This was at a time when people in many parts of the country had lost their land to white settlers, who commandeered the most productive land as property of the Crown or private property. Karuti Kanyinga (2009) demonstrates that the process of alienating Kenyans from their land took place in steps, first with the protectorate acquiring the land, then by the establishment of English property law, endorsing and giving authority to that acquisition. The ancestral and customary recognition of landownership was replaced by Crown laws that privatized ownership by individuals and the colonial state, facilitating the foundation of the settler economy (327). These settlers then used underpaid African labor, especially of men, leaving women, such as Wangari's mother, and children to tend what was left of family land and some women as the only full-time, active parents. Maathai's words and works recognize women as autonomous society members and leaders with agency, a trait she appreciated from her childhood.

The Kenya Land and Freedom Army (KLFA), popularly known as the Mau Mau, responded to this appropriation of native land and loss of freedom by revolting from 1952 until 1956. British officials countered with violence and martial law (Branch 2007; Kanogo 1987; Koster 2014, 2016; Githuku 2015). The beginning of the KLFA uprising and the consequent declaration of the state of emergency by British prime minister Winston Churchill coincided with Wangari's entry into intermediate school after completing her Kenya Primary Examination with extremely high scores at Ihithe Primary School in 1951. She proceeded to boarding school at St. Cecilia's Intermediate Primary School at Mathari, a Catholic mission in Nyeri (Maathai 2007a, 53). Her mother and brother felt that this option held the best promise for her even though the family could ill afford the fees to send her there. This choice would insulate her from the political happenings in the outside world for the time being.

In 1952, then-governor Evelyn Baring declared a state of emergency in Kenya on behalf of the British government and sent British and African soldiers to help colonial administrators capture Mau Mau fighters and send them to detention camps (Heather 2017; Kanogo 1987). It was as part of this campaign that, on April 8, 1953, Jomo Kenyatta, who would become independent Kenya's first prime minister, and then president, was convicted for being a leader of the Mau Mau. He and five others, Bildad Kaggia, Achieng' Oneko, Paul Ngei, Kung'u Karumba, and Fred Kubai, collectively referred to as the Kapenguria Six, were sentenced to seven years with hard labor (Ngesa 2013, 3). Nationalist organizations were under siege, and arrests were rampant. Several members of Wangari's family lost their homes, and some, including her mother, were herded into native reserves or emergency villages as part of this sweep (Maathai 2009a, Kanyinga 2009, 328; Elkins 2000, 36).

The KLFA were very active around Wangari's ancestral home, and members of her family were involved on both sides of the struggle—the revolutionary group or supporters of the home guards, who worked on behalf of the British administration (Maathai 2007a, 64–65). Her time in boarding school ensured that she was spared many of the challenges attached to the uprising. However, as a girl of seventeen, she was picked up while making the trip to Nakuru during her school holidays to visit her father and detained in an emergency village. She was questioned for two days and later released at the intervention of Mr. Neylan. Even though she was insulated from a considerable part of the events, she noted the trauma suffered by others who were not so lucky (65–69). Her time at St. Cecilia's lasted almost the entire duration of the KLFA revolution. She acknowledged that living in the boarding school bubble gave her an inaccurate and tarnished understanding of the KLFA for a long time. She regarded its members as enemies of the people or terrorists, as the British administration characterized them, even praying with others at St. Cecilia's for their defeat (64).

It was also while at St. Cecilia's that Wangari converted to Catholicism and took the name Mary Josephine in honor of Mary and Joseph, the parents of Jesus (Maathai 2007a, 61). Prior to that, as a Protestant, she had been baptized and given the name Miriam (2007b). Even as a young girl, the combination of spiritualities that would inform her philosophy was being nurtured. In this process of spiritual and political sensitization, she remained close to the land, cultivating her plot and communing with its spirituality during her breaks from school (Maathai 2007a, 69).

Entering the Catholic school determined the trajectory of Mary Josephine's future academic journey and would later influence her theorizing and value system. She took the Kenya African Preliminary Examination in 1955 and obtained top marks. In 1956, the same year that she entered Loreto Girls High School in Limuru (a prestigious Catholic school for African girls), the KLFA revolt finally started to wind down, culminating with the seizure of Field Marshal Dedan Kimathi in October (Branch 2010, 203).

Mary Josephine entered young adulthood in a charged political environment, as the nationalist movement was picking up pace across the continent (Maathai 2007a, 73). Kenyatta was released from jail in Lokitaung and placed under house arrest in Lodwar in 1959 (Nyangena 2003, 4), the same year she graduated from Loreto. She excelled in the Cambridge School Certificate examinations, earning a first division. On January 12, 1960, the state of emergency officially ended, and Britain announced plans to prepare Kenya for majority African governance. This was the Kenya that Mary Josephine left behind on her first trip out of the country as part of the Kennedy Airlift project, in which Kenyans received scholarships to study at universities in the United States (Nyangena 2003, 73; Speich 2009, 455). The initiative, spearheaded by Tom Mboya and US senator John F. Kennedy, was an investment in young East Africans who would help build the postindependence nations. The Catholic Church in Kenya looked to the leading Catholic schools for candidates to participate in the program. Having just graduated with excellent results, Mary Josephine Wangari was an obvious choice. She made the decision to give up an opportunity to study at Makerere University in Kampala, then the premier East African university, and at twenty years of age, Mary Josephine Wangari traveled to the United States to begin her college education at Mount St. Scholastica College in Atchison, Kansas. A series of adjustments would mark not just her life but also that of her country over the ten years that followed.

In 1961, Jomo Kenyatta was released after years of detention, hard labor, and house arrest and assumed the presidency of the political party Kenya African National Union (KANU). In 1963, Kenya gained independence, with Kenyatta elected prime minister on May 27. On June 1, 1963, commemorated as Madaraka Day, Kenya's first self-governing administration was established, also achieving internal self-rule. Kenya became officially independent in December 1963, and the republic was formed on December 12, 1964, with Kenyatta as its first president. Years later, Maathai recalled, "For me, it was a moment to celebrate that finally we were free, as Martin Luther King was crying out at that time. I thought we were going to enjoy our freedom, we were going to be happy, we were not going to be oppressed anymore. Little did I know what lay ahead" (2005c, 39). Maathai's combined experiences—of colonialism, the plight of colonized Africans, Kenyans' agitation for independence, the postindependence situation for Kenyans and especially women, the conditions of African Americans in the United States, and the civil rights era—informed the development of her ideas and ideals, politics and activism. Regarding the civil rights movement, she said, "It shaped my concept of human rights, and it made me understand that human rights are not things that are put on the table for people to enjoy. These are things you fight for, and then you protect" (2009a).

In 1964, Mary Josephine earned her bachelor of science degree in biology from Mount St. Scholastica and proceeded to the University of Pittsburgh for graduate studies. Back in Kenya, the National Council of Women of Kenya (NCWK) was established as the institution that would coordinate activities of women's groups and associations. As Kenya had moved toward independence, organizations formerly run by colonial wives and other white women had started handing over the reins to Kenyan women. These included Maendeleo ya

Wanawake (MYWO), an organization Maathai would later be a part of and then at odds with, which elected its first African president in 1961. The NCWK was expressly founded to oversee some of these organizations. Maathai later led the NCWK, under whose banner she started the Green Belt Movement (GBM). The NCWK would later launch her into national politics in the 1980s. In 1962, the Kenya Association of University Women (KAUW) was founded as an affiliate of the International Federation of University Women (later renamed Graduate Women International [GWI]). The KAUW, whose membership consisted of women with university degrees from recognized institutions, would propel Maathai into the political and activist spotlight and enable her membership in the NCWK.

As this flurry of political, social, and civic developments related to gender picked up momentum in Kenya, Mary Jo was focused on earning her master of science degree in biological sciences from the University of Pittsburgh, which she did in January 1966. Her thesis, titled "Developmental and Cytological Study of the Pineal Body of *Coturnix coturnix japonica*," was adjudged "excellent" by the examining board (Maathai 2007a, 95). Toward the completion of her master's degree, recruiters from the University College of Nairobi interviewed her in Pittsburgh and followed up with a job offer, asking her to report for duty on January 10, 1966.

Mary Jo returned on January 6, 1966, to a nation and continent where many changes had occurred. Her intention was to take up the position of research assistant to a professor of zoology at the University College of Nairobi, as outlined in her job offer letter. However, upon reporting to work on January 10, she was informed that her promised job had been offered to someone else, which she believed was due to gender and ethnic bias (Maathai 2007a, 100–101). This marked a significant turning point in her career as an academic. She eventually found work under Professor Reinhold Hofmann in the microanatomy section of the newly established Department of Veterinary Anatomy in the School of Veterinary Medicine at the University College of Nairobi.

Two other significant changes happened in 1966. She dropped her "English" names, preferring to go again by her Gikuyu name, Wangari, and she met her future husband, Mwangi Mathai. The name change was part of a conscious embracing of her indigenous Gikuyu and African self that began the disposition of unapologetic Africanness one encounters in her work, words, and self-fashioning. She recounted her shifting sensibilities, specifically on self-identifying and the duality of names and consciousness, in a 2007 interview at the Museum of Natural History in Washington, DC, saying, "Later on when I went to school and became a Christian, you were told to adopt a new name, and you were told to accept that as your first name. But it is actually your second name" (2007b). She offered the example of the fact that in Kansas she was addressed as Miss Wangari, which was when she started deconstructing the question of names and naming. She shared a realization about her various name changes: "I had been walking in a zig zag way and I decided to go back to the beginning, and I said, "My name is Wangari!" I decided that from then on, I would try to look at myself using my own mirror and would not allow people to tell me who I was" (2007b).

Wangari Muta started her doctoral studies with encouragement from Professor Hofmann and relocated to Germany on a scholarship under the Nairobi-Giessen partnership program in 1967 to pursue doctoral research and training from the University of Giessen and the University of Munich. At the time there was only one electron microscope in Kenya. Because more were expected to arrive at Kenyan universities, she spent part of her time in Germany extending her experience working with this equipment (Maathai 2007a, 107). In 1969, after twenty months in Germany, she returned to Kenya to the position of assistant lecturer at the University College of Nairobi and to complete her PhD dissertation. In what was a busy year, she married Mwangi Mathai and was immediately thrown into her role as a politician's wife during his unsuccessful campaign for a seat in parliament.

This was a year of personal and national turmoil. Wangari Mathai experienced great personal loss with the passing of her brother Kibicho, the assassination of government minister Tom Mboya triggered ethnic unrest, and Kenya also became a de facto one-party state after the Kenya People's Union (KPU) was banned. The KPU's leader, Oginga Odinga, was arrested, leaving KANU the only party to "compete" in the elections. Later, in the 1970s through the 1990s, this situation would heavily impact Maathai's politics and political engagements. It also directly impacted the place of her husband in politics and thus Wangari Mathai's social location. This was the Kenya of her post-Germany return, in which she quickly found her place and voice in her roles as career woman, wife, and mother.

Wangari Muta Mathai completed her PhD dissertation, titled "Early Development of Male Bovine Gonad," in 1970, the year her first son, Waweru, was born. She was awarded a degree in anatomy from the University College of Nairobi in 1971 (Maathai 2007a, 112), the year she gave birth to her daughter, Wanjira. Wangari Mathai was the first woman in East and Central Africa to receive a doctoral degree. She rejoined the faculty at the university as senior lecturer of anatomy. In 1974, her second son, Muta, was born, and her husband won the parliamentary elections to become the member of parliament (MP) for Lang'ata Constituency. Here began her more active public life and advocacy, informed and motivated by her identities as academic, mother, and public servant.

Even as she supported her husband's political career, her own professional journey witnessed an upward trajectory in the mid-1970s. She became a senior lecturer in anatomy in 1975, chair of the Department of Veterinary Anatomy in 1976, and in 1977 she was promoted to associate professor (Maathai 2007a, 118). She was the first African woman in the department to hold those positions, all while enduring and fighting against constant gender bias from both students and faculty members, including some who openly or indirectly questioned her competence. Outside the university, she worked for various civic organizations, including the KAUW and the local Environment Liaison Centre. In 1974, she was invited to serve on the board of the latter, and, from 1973 to 1980, she served as director of the Nairobi branch of the Kenya Red Cross (119).

It was in this season of her life that her interests and work began to coalesce. When her husband became an MP, Wangari Mathai facilitated the fulfillment of promises he had made to his constituents during the campaign period. Mwangi Mathai had pledged to increase employment opportunities for his constituents to alleviate skyrocketing unemployment. She shared in her memoir that after winning the elections he dropped the plan, which had been just a strategic campaign promise. She wanted to fulfill the incomplete contract her husband had entered into with his constituents. Thus, Wangari Mathai founded her first environment-related organization, Envirocare. The company not only intended to provide employment but also to attend to environmental restoration. Envirocare's first nursery was erected in the Karura Forest. However, due to financial hitches and lack of support from her husband, once she moved the nursery production to their home, the project shut down (Maathai 2007a, 127–29). Nevertheless, her efforts did not go unnoticed. The United Nations Environment Program (UNEP) sponsored her trip to the June 1976 United Nations Conference on Human Settlements, also known as

Habitat I, in Vancouver, Canada, where participants called for greener cities, among other recommendations. The trip to Habitat I was a major turning point, launching Wangari Mathai on a journey that solidified her position as a scholar and activist on matters of women's rights and empowerment, the environment, and governance. Because she was a member of the KAUW, Wangari Mathai had joined the NCWK. When she returned to Nairobi after Habitat I, the NCWK invited her to speak about the conference and its deliberations. Out of this presentation and the ensuing action plans, a new idea and program was born, committed to reforestation and saving the environment. The organization approved the idea and established the Save the Land Harambee project (Maathai 2007a, 131). On June 5, 1977, to celebrate World Environment Day, the NCWK and Save the Land Harambee organized a march to Kamukunji Grounds in Nairobi, where they planted seven trees in honor of seven Kenyan (s)heroes: Wangu wa Makeri, Waiyaki wa Hinga, Mekatilili wa Menza, Masaku Ngei, Nabongo Mumia, Ole Lenana, and Gor Mahia wuod Ogalo. Save the Land Harambee was the forerunner of the GBM (119–25). Both, albeit cash strapped, operated as successful components of the NCWK.

Wangari Mathai's personal life, at the time, was not progressing as well as her public one. In 1977, she and her husband separated, and in 1979 Mwangi Mathai filed for divorce. The three-week divorce proceedings in court turned ugly. Whereas some have reported that Mwangi sought divorce on the grounds that she was too uncontrollable and strong-minded, Wangari maintained that he falsely claimed she had been unfaithful and contributed to the deterioration of his health (Maathai 2007a, 145–46). The case ended with a win for him and new troubles for her. In an interview with Salim Lone of *Viva* magazine following the ruling, she stated that the judge would have had to be corrupt or incompetent to render that judgment. The judge then threatened her with a contempt-of-court charge if she did not withdraw the statement. She refused to back down and was charged and found guilty. Sentenced to six months in prison, she was taken to Lang'ata Women's Prison without the opportunity to say goodbye or explain the situation to her children. After three days, her lawyer negotiated a deal wherein she wrote a statement the court found sufficient, setting her free (147–50).

Most know Wangari Maathai as a radical outspoken activist. She questioned whether her life would have taken the same trajectory had she stayed married to Mwangi (*Taking Root*). Following the divorce, Mwangi demanded that she drop his name, and she made the bold choice to change it by adding an extra *a*, becoming Wangari Muta Maathai. Her life at this time also underwent other weighty changes. The court case, lawyer's fees, and the fact that she had decided not to ask for support from Mwangi left her in financial difficulties (Maathai 2007a, 152–53). Additionally, she had to relocate to a new house with her children. Struggling to make ends meet, she accepted an offer from the United Nations Development Program (UNDP) to work as a consultant for six months in Lusaka, Zambia, with the Economic Commission for Africa. Upon reaching that decision, she loaded up the kids in the car, drove to Mwangi's house unannounced, and dropped them off, promising to return in a little while. She failed to explain that the "little while" would be six months. The children would stay with Mwangi until 1985, when they came back to stay with her of their own volition.

Meanwhile, events in the Kenyan political sphere further stimulated the development of her public persona. While her marriage was deteriorating, on August, 22, 1978, Jomo Kenyatta passed away and was succeeded by Daniel arap Moi. This ushered in a period of adverse interactions between Maathai and Moi as his presidency produced conditions that required more radical responses from activists. Her personal contestations with him started with her interest in the position of chair of the NCWK at the annual elections in 1979. She ran for the post that year but lost by three votes and served for a year as vice chair.

The following year, when she ran for chair again, the government, not wanting her to serve, interfered openly with the elections through representatives of the NCWK's largest member organization, the MYWO. The government representatives expected the MYWO to take charge by making the case that the NCWK was an organization for elite women that was disconnected from grassroots women and who could not understand their needs or represent their interests. Even with this interference, Maathai won the election (Maathai 2007a, 157–58), and she would be reelected year after year until 1987, when she did not run for office. Her initial win caused the government to pull support for the NCWK, forcing members to find other ways to fund their operations and initiatives. Further, the MYWO withdrew from the NCWK, and the government directed most support toward women's initiatives through the former. Despite these roadblocks and immense financial problems, the NCWK gained local and global visibility for its work on the environment, development, and women's empowerment under Maathai's leadership.

The 1980s were tough yet defining years for Maathai. At a time when she was struggling to rebuild her life after the divorce, she started her seven-year service as chair of the NCWK. Moi's power increased in 1982 when, following a failed coup attempt, the president and his government pushed through a constitutional amendment to make Kenya a de jure one-party state, although it had been so, de facto, since 1969. The hyperauthoritarian president grew steadily more intolerant of any opposition, and this informed his relationship with Maathai for years to come. The government heightened its suppression of detractors and opposition leaders, a situation that would endure through the decade, leading to the exiling of many Kenyans, including academics and artists such as Micere Githae Mugo, Ngugi wa Thiong'o, and Wangari wa Goro. The attempted coup drew the country's ethnic political identifying lines sharper as Oginga Odinga and his son Raila Odinga were implicated in it, with Raila placed in detention for six years.

It was during this decade that Maathai's political identity came into focus, fueling her radical activism. In 1982, Maathai gave up her position at the University of Nairobi to run for a parliamentary seat, but she was blocked from running on a technicality, which she contested in court. The University of Nairobi, whose chancellor was President Moi, declined to offer her back her job, which she had left only three days earlier, stating that it had been given to someone else (Maathai 2007a, 162). As Vertistine Mbaya, a board member at the GBM and a close personal friend of Maathai's, remembered, Maathai had nothing left to lose, and this heightened the lengths to which she was willing to go in her advocacy (*Taking Root* 2008).

Without a job, she settled in as the only full-time worker and co-ordinator for the GBM, an unsalaried position. Eventually, funding from the Norwegian Forestry Society, the Voluntary Fund for the United Nations Decade for Women, and the Norwegian Agency for Development Cooperation (NORAD) allowed the GBM to expand its programs and staff, and Maathai stayed on as coordinator, ending her job hunt. Having one leader for both the GBM and the NCWK at the same time provided prime opportunities for the two organizations to feed each other's missions and projects. For Maathai, it was an opportunity to fine-tune her ideas and ideals on questions of women's rights, environmentalism, and governance.

Maathai's public persona as a political, gender, and environmental activist and as a critical thinker continued to grow even as the Moi administration intensified its crackdown on government critics, often inciting global criticism for political arrests and human rights abuses. So intense was the state's focus on Maathai that she encouraged her children to move to the United States for their safety and to continue their studies (Maathai 2007a, 155). The conflict between Maathai and the government on the plans to erect the Times Media Trust Complex Tower, a sixty-story skyscraper, and a statue of Moi at Uhuru Park in Nairobi, chronicled in chapter 4, intensified this animosity. Following this event, the GBM was evicted from the government offices it occupied, and she moved all GBM operations to her house in the South C neighborhood in Nairobi, where it was located until 1996.

The work of the GBM became progressively intertwined with the work of the prodemocracy movement, and Maathai became an outspoken advocate for a democratic Kenya. The 1988 elections left many Kenyans unhappy, and as the 1990s approached, agitation for democratic governance was on the rise. The murder of Foreign Affairs Minister Robert Ouko in February 1990 sparked more dissent against the government, emboldening the prodemocracy movement, which was calling for a return to multiparty politics. The Saba Saba prodemocracy meeting at Kamukunji on July 7, 1990, which organizers proceeded with despite the fact that they had been denied a license, was violently disrupted by police (Muigai 1993, 27). That day, 7/7, would become known in Kenyan history as Saba Saba Day (*saba* being "seven" in Kiswahili) and remains a significant marker in the journey toward a democratic Kenya. The events of that day galvanized more Kenyans to stand behind the struggle for democracy and captivated the world's attention. Maathai, later, planted trees at Uhuru Park to memorialize the victims who died on the day. After Saba Saba, she remained a constant fixture in what would become known as Kenya's second liberation. In turn, the Moi regime continued to monitor her activities closely, increasing its hostility toward the GBM as the 1990s began. During these years, Maathai was constantly afraid for her life. She reflected, "I realized that I was now a political figure, and that I had to take care even as I knew I couldn't stay silent" (2007a, 206–7).

The 1990s constituted the most radical years of the prodemocracy and women's movements in Kenya up to that point. This volatile time was characterized by expanding prodemocracy initiatives, protests, and battles; outbreaks of ethnic violence related to elections; and the fight for affirmative action on behalf of Kenya's women. Against this setting, Maathai's global profile and visibility as an activist for human rights, democracy, women's rights, and environmental protection expanded. Some saw her as a liberator and others as an anti(s)hero. Her crusading resulted in public judgment and shaming, repeat imprisonments and assaults, and reported assassination threats.

The crusaders for Kenya's second liberation challenged section 2A of the constitution, even demanding a dissolution of parliament. As part of this campaign, in August 1991, six opposition leaders, Oginga Odinga, Masinde Muliro, Martin Shikuku, Philip Gachoka, Ahmed Bamahriz and George Nthenge, formed the Forum for the Restoration of Democracy (FORD) and invited the participation of like-minded individuals, including Professor Maathai (Muigai 1993, 29). The government reacted by outlawing the party and arresting its members but released them following criticism from local and global leaders and governments, including those of the United States and United Kingdom (29). At the time, the agenda of the women's movement was becoming intertwined with the prodemocracy movement, placing Maathai at the center of the action as a principal of both movements. As 1991 wound down, the Paris Club made the decision to freeze aid to Kenya until change was evident in policy and practice, a direct result of the unrelenting campaigns by the leaders of the prodemocracy movement as well as increased international scrutiny of Kenya's poor democratic practices, human rights violations, and economic mismanagement (28). This was a significant blow to the Kenyan government. The reality that many African nations— Cape Verde, São Tomé and Príncipe, Zambia, Benin, Burkina Faso, Guinea-Bissau, the Central African Republic, Mauritania, Rwanda, and Madagascar—were embracing multipartyism around the same time put extra pressure toward change on the Moi regime.

On December 3, 1991, a special KANU conference at the Kasarani Sports Complex in Nairobi agreed to the reintroduction of multiparty politics and the legalization of opposition parties. On December 10, the amendment to the constitution repealing section 2A, marking transition from a one-party system to a return to multiparty politics in Kenya, was passed in parliament (Adar and Munyae 2001, 8). Multipartyism opened up opportunities to engage semiliberally in opposition politics. In July 1992, female delegates at the National Capacity Building Workshop for women candidates, hosted by the National Committee on the Status of Women–Kenya (NCSW), endorsed

Wangari Maathai as the women's choice for president of Kenya. She declined the invitation to run, however, preferring to focus on her work with the GBM and with grassroots women.

The rise of opposition politics in Kenya came up against a militantly obdurate government, leading to a bloody march toward democratization. Maathai and other members of FORD spent much of the 1990s in running battles with the government. Unfortunately, in 1992, FORD split into two parties—FORD-Kenya, led by Oginga Odinga, and FORD-Asili, led by Kenneth Matiba. Splintering the opposition further, Mwai Kibaki and John Keen founded the Democratic Party of Kenya (Fox 1996, 601). As part of her work with the prodemocracy movement, Maathai cofounded and served as chair of the Middle Ground Group (MGG), tasked with reuniting the opposition, and also led the Movement for Free and Fair Elections (Allen 1997, 332–33). Because the GBM was an active partner in these initiatives, detractors often lumped the activities and criticism of the two movements together. Thus, as Maathai's stature as an environmentalist grew internationally, so did her politically instigated conflicts back in Kenya. This was demonstrated in the 1992 Release Political Prisoners (RPP) protest and, later, the globally publicized fight to save the indigenous Karura Forest. These events, explored further in chapter 3 and appendix 2 respectively, placed her in direct conflict with Moi and his government. The run-ins with the government were accompanied by assaults, hospitalizations, arrests, court appearances, death threats, and constant intimidation for crusaders for democracy.

Global leaders and organizations, including the secretary-general of the United Nations (UN), leaders of Western nations, religious leaders, Amnesty International, and Human Rights Watch, would intervene time and again to ensure the safety of Maathai and other prodemocracy leaders (Maathai 2007a). With direct threats made against her life, Maathai later recounted that she often had to travel during the night and in disguise and even change cars to avoid detection on her trips. She regularly stayed at safe houses she and her friends and supporters had established (247).

The administration's antagonism toward Maathai and the risks to her life are exemplified by events relating to a planned seminar in Nakuru on ethnic violence that followed the 1992 elections. She reported that she, with GBM employees and other partners, were engaged in initiatives toward establishing peace and rebuilding communities following conflict in the Rift Valley. On this particular occasion, members of the police force with guns and dogs blocked their entry to the venue of the proceedings. Fearing for her life, she arranged to ride back to Nairobi with an ambassador of a foreign nation to ensure her security. Government representatives foiled further attempts to hold the event and other meetings in the Rift Valley, forcing Maathai to file an injunction with the High Court to compel the government to cease the obstructive behavior toward her efforts to convene the seminar (Maathai 2007a, 238–42).

In this environment, on February 23, 1993, one of Maathai's allies, Dr. Ngorongo Makanga, was abducted from his pharmacy, and Maathai reported receiving death threats. In an open letter to the attorney general, she requested protection and followed this with a trip on March 4 to the courthouse to plead bail before arrest in an effort to preempt any attempts to take her into custody. The following day, she went into hiding for two months after sending out a call for international organizations and governments to uphold the freezing of aid that had been instituted against the country before Kenya's transition back to multipartyism (Maathai 2007a, 244–46). On that same day, Amnesty International published the statement "Fear for Safety KENYA: Wangari Maathai (female)—Environmentalist, Opposition Activist," calling for appeals demanding the guaranteed safety of Maathai and Dr. Makanga to be sent to President Moi, Commissioner of Police Phillip Kilonzo, and Attorney General Amos Wako.

As previously mentioned, Maathai's security was made possible by supporters, including friends, prodemocracy leaders and activists, foreign diplomats, and religious leaders. Vertistine Mbaya recalled, "We were constantly on the lookout to make sure they didn't pick her up, particularly secretly where nobody could protest because that's when the damage can be done" (*Taking Root* 2008). On March 17, 1993, eight female politicians made a public statement asking the president to stop trying to intimidate Maathai. On April 18, Mikhail Gorbachev sent President Moi a letter requesting that he personally guarantee her safety as she traveled to the first International Green Cross gathering in Kyoto, Japan, which the former president of the Soviet Union had founded (Maathai 2007a, 248). Moi denied that the government was harassing Maathai, asserting that she was free to come and go as she pleased. The next day, she came out of hiding.

That June, Maathai attended and spoke at the UN's World Conference on Human Rights in Vienna, where she also planned to hold an exhibition of photos on the ethnic violence in Kenya and distribute the parliamentary report on the violence. She later disclosed that persons acting on behalf of the government had stolen the photos and reports. This act of sabotage, she noted, was not an isolated event. She had helped establish the Tribal Clashes Resettlement Volunteer Service to support rebuilding postconflict communities (*Taking Root* 2008, 238), and government forces had constantly inhibited its efforts. The following September, Maathai called a press conference to say that she planned to sue the government for failing to intervene to stop the ethnic violence in Kenya. According to the Human Rights Watch Africa, approximately fifteen hundred Kenyans lost their lives and three hundred thousand were internally displaced during these ethnic conflicts (Materu 2014, 38). Lack of government will and investment in addressing the core issues related to ethnic conflicts resulted in violence flaring again briefly in some parts of the country in 1994.

As prodemocracy leaders intensified the call for a functioning democracy, the vigilance of the government against any criticism heightened. Supporters of the opposition were forced to apply for licenses to hold meetings, which were habitually denied. Defiant, the movement's leaders sometimes held the meetings anyway, resulting in numerous arrests. Political trials for treason and sedition became the order of the day. Maathai and the MGG continued their work through 1993 and 1994, often holding meetings at her house late into the night. Maathai reminisced in her memoir, *Unbowed,* "We held seminars in my house in the evenings, since during the day the house resembled a beehive, packed with Green Belt staff. People came over and sat in the living room and I'd teach, sometimes until one or two o'clock in the morning. . . . At this time, we were still being constantly monitored by government informers" (2007a, 250).

On October 1, 1993, the pressure from the movements for democracy and women's rights compelled the government to appoint a task force led by Justice Effie Awuor to review laws and customs relating to women. During its tenure, the task force would contribute to the drafting of bills that included the Equality Bill, the Affirmative Action Bill, the Family Protection Bill, and the Gender Policy Bill. As the first half of the decade wound down, Maathai and other Kenyan and African female leaders focused on preparations for the UN's Fourth World Conference on Women, to be held in Beijing in 1995. It is important to note here that over four decades she worked closely with other champions of the postindependence women's movement in Kenya. These sister-activists who influenced and were influenced by Maathai include Micere Mugo, Muthoni Likimani, Eddah Gachukia, Grace Onyango, Jane Kiano, Ida Odinga, Wanjiru Kabiru, Margaret Kenyatta, Achola Pala, Maria Nzomo, and Tabitha Seii. The organizations affiliated with the women's movement in Kenya focused in the 1990s on building broader, stronger regional and global networks to fight for basic human rights and political inclusion for women. From November 16 to 23, 1994, the Fifth Regional Conference on Women was held in Dakar, where the African Platform for Action was adopted in readiness for Beijing. In the summer of 1995, Maathai convened, with the NCWK, a conference in Nairobi, also in preparation for Beijing (Maathai 2007a, 252; Chegu and Wamahiu 1999, 417). At the Beijing conference on August 30, 1995, she presented the paper "Bottlenecks to Development in Africa." The spirit of the paper demonstrates why activities of the women's movement following the Beijing conference were inextricably linked to the activities of the prodemocracy movement in Kenya. The paper also highlights the interconnections between global human rights and the challenges that Africans and their nations faced. This is illustrative of her holistic and utu-based approach to engaging knowledge and activism.

The prodemocracy movement picked up steam during the second multiparty elections in 1997. On November 20, 1997, five weeks before the elections, Maathai announced that she would be running for president under the banner of the Liberal Party of Kenya in an election that included fifteen presidential candidates. The party was later renamed the Mazingira Green Party of Kenya, with a focus on promoting green values. The organization eventually became a member of the Green Parties of Africa and the global network of green parties. She reported that on the eve of the election, a rumor had circulated, with the help of the media, that she had withdrawn her candidacy for the presidency and the parliamentary seat. It was unclear whether this had any effect on her numbers in the election. The blow of a second win by Moi in multiparty elections was massive for the prodemocracy movement and the women's movement. At the same time, it motivated and galvanized support for both movements as the twentieth century came to a close.

Even as Maathai doubled down as a key player in both movements, the turn of the century was consumed with taking care of her mother, who passed away on International Women's Day in 2000 (Maathai

2007a, 274). Maathai also immersed herself in activism against global economic systems that disadvantaged African countries. This work, including her service to the Jubilee 2000 Africa Campaign, is engaged in chapter 5. While her journey from 2001 to 2010 was still loaded with battles for democracy, justice, human rights, and environmental conservation, this was in many ways a winning decade for Maathai. She took up fellowships—Montgomery Fellow at Dartmouth College in 2001 and Dorothy McCluskey Visiting Fellow for Conservation at Yale University in 2002. Significantly, on the home front through the decade, the role of Wangari Maathai and others of the prodemocracy movement led to the realization of a new constitution in 2010 (Kramon and Posner 2011, 89; Kanyinga and Long 2012, 41). Additionally, Moi's twenty-four-year rule ended in the presidential election of December 27, 2002, when Mwai Kibaki, the head of an opposition coalition, the National Rainbow Alliance (NARC), won. Maathai earned a seat in parliament to represent the Tetu Constituency in Nyeri District after receiving 98 percent of the vote as a NARC candidate. On December 30, Kibaki took power, and in January 2003, he appointed Maathai assistant minister in the Ministry of Environment and Natural Resources.

Many critiqued her lack of impact on government policies and structures in relation to the environment during her tenure, a situation some argue was contributed to by the fact that she was an assistant minister and not the minister. Over the decade, uplifted by the African Union's passing of the Protocol on the Rights of Women in Africa, the new female parliamentarians, including Maathai, delivered an active women-focused agenda in Kenya's parliament.

In 2004, Professor Wangari Maathai was awarded the Nobel Peace Prize for her efforts toward realizing "sustainable development, democracy and peace" (Norwegian Nobel Committee, 2004). This was the most significant but only one of a plethora of prestigious awards she received, a list of which is included in appendix 1.

In that same year, Maathai did an interview with *Time* magazine, in which she was widely reported as having claimed that HIV/AIDS was an agent created by the West to decimate African populations. She subsequently denied this in an interview with Pal Amitabh in the *Progressive Interview*, stating, "I never said what was being reported, and I don't believe in it. . . . I don't know why the reporter reported that, and I noticed that even though I kept saying that I didn't say that, the reporter still continued to report what he wanted to report. . . . I am sorry that people got me completely wrong" (Maathai 2005c). Elsewhere (Maathai 2004b), she sought to clarify, saying, "I have . . . been shocked by the ongoing debate generated by what I am purported to have said. It is therefore critical for me to state that I neither say nor believe that the virus was developed by white people or white powers in order to destroy the African people. Such views are wicked and destructive." Her statements failed to put this controversy to bed successfully, and it continues to plague her legacy.

After receiving the Nobel Peace Prize, while she remained active in her roles within Kenya, Maathai also took on prominence and responsibilities that were more regional and global in nature, as chronicled in appendix 1. In 2006, she collaborated with sister laureates Jody Williams, Shirin Ebadi, Rigoberta Menchú Tum, Betty Williams, and Mairead Maguire to start the Nobel Women Initiative, with the aim of promoting peace and equity. The laureates consolidated their experiences and vast influential platforms to bring attention to challenges of grassroots women across the world as well as to support their work and promote various initiatives and movements.

In 2007, Maathai lost her bid to return to parliament and continued to work as an ambassador for human rights, women's rights, democracy, and environmental protection globally. During the postelection violence in 2007–8, she joined mediation teams to promote unity and peace through restorative justice approaches, as she had done after the 2002 elections. She maintained her work with the GBM, which established new initiatives, including the Women and Girls project. To crown it all, in 2010, she helped establish the Wangari Maathai Institute for Peace and Environmental Studies (WMI),[1] housed at the same veterinary campus at the University of Nairobi where she had lost her job (S. G. Kiama,[2] personal communication with author, July 11, 2018). The establishment of this institution, which grants master's and doctoral degrees, represented a full-circle return of Maathai the scholar, with her academic and activist ideals and ideas infused into the development of an entire academic institution. She served as WMI's founding distinguished chair, a position she held until she passed away on September 25, 2011, at the age of seventy-one, following a battle with ovarian cancer.

Wangari Muta Maathai was mourned globally. To honor her commitment to environmental protection, "her remains were placed in a bamboo-frame coffin made of water hyacinth and papyrus reeds. She was cremated, and her remains were interred in the compound of the Wangari Maathai Institute for Peace and Environmental Studies" (Dalby 2011).

This chapter has explored the roots of Maathai's individualities related to environmental development and management, women's rights, human rights, democratic politics, and international relations as developed out of interactions with particular personal, Kenyan, and global histories. These identities are numerous and complex. As a scholar and academic leader, this first female PhD in East and Central Africa (and awardee of over fifteen honorary doctorates) was a scientist, researcher, professor, author of books, public intellectual, department chair, and distinguished academic chair. As an activist, she was an environmental conservationist, a human rights defender, an advocate for peace, a UN messenger of peace, a global feminist, a board member for various organizations, a philanthropist, and a goodwill ambassador. As a politician, she was a presidential candidate, a political party leader, an assistant minister, an MP, an activist for democracy, and a thorn in the side of the oppressive Kenyan government as well as global governance bodies. Her thoughts and philosophies that emerged from these interfacing identities, roles, and histories, and which epitomize her ideas and ideals, are explored in the chapters that follow.

2

Replenishing the Earth

Maathai's Holistic Environmentalism

This chapter focuses on Wangari Maathai's critical thoughts and philosophies on the subject of environmental conservation, articulated in *Replenishing the Earth: Spiritual Values for Healing Ourselves and the World* (2010) and *The Green Belt Movement: Sharing the Approach and the Experience* (2003) as well as her lectures, speeches, articles, interviews, and activist exercises. I abstract from these a conceptualization of holistic environmentalism that offers a path to sustainable environmental (re)production, protection, and justice, which serves as a path to other forms of social justice. Maathai's critical ideas analyzed in the four sections of this chapter exemplify her trademark holistic environmentalism that is rooted in radical utu. The first and second sections systemize what she considered the necessary jumping-off point for any efforts at environmental defense work: an understanding of and appreciation for the state of the environment. As she reasoned, "The immediate response to the crisis is the rainfall has not come. 'The rains did not come.' But very few of us ask, 'Why didn't the rains come?' That's the challenge. We need to ask ourselves, and that's why we're being challenged to think holistically" (Maathai 2005b). Maathai suggested that the practice of holistic environmentalism requires approaches based on a comprehensive understanding of specific environments, and this demands a shift in outlooks and approaches in the study of ecologies. In the first section, I cover the lenses and perspectives she proposed for reading environments and the entities and interactions within those environments. These perspectives would be incomplete without historicizing localized states of environments, as I demonstrate in the second section, using Maathai's analysis of Kenya's environmental history.

Proficiency and familiarity with the state of the environment informs the development of critical approaches for investigating environmental issues and environmentalism as well as appropriate and effective models for practical conservationism. In sections three and four, I present the processes that follow the acquisition of the insights identified above—that is, the definition of environmentalist knowledge construction and activist models. The principles articulated in Maathai's work and delineated in these sections endorse the designing of approaches for environmentalism, which serve both the physical world and the human beings residing in it. Apposite and well-directed conservationism, for Maathai, was difficult to achieve without clear foundational values and ideals. The frameworks that emerge from this examination of her work and words center the ideal that environmental management exists in synergetic relationships with other processes and realities, including peace, security, health, capacity building, and poverty reduction. It is through this filter that she conceptualized conservation, environmental justice, and ecological security not only as bound to but also as a route to ensuring other types of security, including food, human, and national.

Translation of these ideas and ideals into active radical environmentalism is made possible by the processes and frameworks described. Maathai named environmental protection and replenishing as political acts, conceptualizing the act of planting trees as a symbol of defiance (Maathai 2006). Teasing out this idea, I complete the chapter by focalizing applications of Maathai's critical thoughts and values toward activating what I call utu-driven eco-revolutions.

Utu and Cognizing Environments

Desmond Tutu deciphers, "Africa is the birthplace of *ubuntu*, the ancient spirituality of humanity, oneness with our creator, the other, and nature. Together with humanity's team, I dream of a new world and a new humanity—a humanity that expresses *ubuntu. Umuntu ngumuntu ngabantu*—I am because we are. We are all one" (2012). Per this definition, the human condition and the condition of being human are intimately connected to humans' relationship with their environment. Maathai's holistic environmentalism is inseparable from utu. She said, "Human beings have a consciousness by which we can appreciate love, beauty, creativity, and innovation or mourn the lack thereof. To the extent that we can go beyond ourselves and ordinary biological instincts, we experience what it means to be human and therefore different from other forms of life" (Maathai 2010a, 17). Maathai offered a deeper environmental dimension to the beingness of the human, arguing, "In degrading the environment, therefore, we degrade ourselves and all humankind" (17). To wit, we lose some of our humanity, with damage happening at physical, psychological, and spiritual levels when our environment is mutilated. This stresses the criticality of human beings appreciating the coadjuvant nature of their relationship with the environment so they can develop appropriate ways of interacting with that environment. Such development and awareness can only nurture and further heighten their humanness—their utu.

Maathai defined and situated "the source," ever present in the environment, as a place of knowledge and awareness, which should inform how human beings as individuals and collectives interact with their environments (Maathai 2010, 21–22). In this conceptualization, the association between the environment and the human is sacred and symbiotic. In Maathai's view, "if we can't or won't assist in the earth's healing process, the planet might not take care of us either" (24). In the books *Replenishing the Earth, Unbowed: A Memoir* (2007), and *The Challenge for Africa* (2009), she stressed that the relationship between humans and their environment, across cultures, has always had deeply spiritual dimensions. Thus, interfaces with nature provide symbiotic healing on two levels and connect human beings to their physical and spiritual selves, whatever they define those to be, and, as a consequence, their humanity and all humanity. According to Maathai, for environmental and human rescue to be activated, individuals must meet their responsibility to their environments for themselves, their communities, and future generations locally and globally. Maathai's philosophy of environmentalism, therefore, is rooted in a universal utu (Maathai 2010a, 16–17), which triggers and sustains holistic thinking. Below, I outline the changes in perspectives she conceptualized to inform this way of being and knowing.

Maathai proposed a tridimensional approach to understanding the environment, which combined application of the big-picture perspective (thinking universally) and the long-view perspective (considering the environment over time), working in tandem with a consideration for the small and the local. She rationalized the big-picture perspective's capacity to "open up deeper inquiries as to our relationship to the planet, and force us to ask questions about our attitude toward it and activities upon it—questions that, in the rush of our day-to-day lives, where we do not see our effect on the whole, we may not be able to grasp the significance of'" (Maathai 2010a, 61). Maathai was quick to elaborate that the big picture can be realized at different layers beyond the individual space and person, from one's local space to the earth as a whole. The long view's vertical perspective of space and horizontal perspective of time "offer only more wonder and astonishment: at the magnitude of created existence, and the awesome responsibility we humans have in not only comprehending it, but protecting what we can" (64).

Losing sight of the big picture and the long view has had significant ramifications (Maathai 2010a, 64–67). Maathai described a dissonance in experiential understanding across generations, which compromises possibilities for collective action to save the environment as well as cross-generational passing-on of environmental knowledge and history. Using the example of central Kenya, she observed that her generation was able to recognize the degradation that had occurred to the environment with the loss of the thick forests and functioning waterways and the ecosystems they supported. On the other hand, to the youth, the dense tea and coffee plantations signal healthy, thriving environments—this is the central Kenya of their lifelong experience, and so even the drying streams are acceptable as part of this backdrop because this has always been the limit of their experience with their environment (64–65). Failing to recognize the big-picture and long-view perspectives also causes short memories in relation to changing environmental conditions. For example, after long, devastating droughts, as soon as the rains fall, communities appear to have collective amnesia about the drought, and so little effort is put toward preventing a recurrence. This leads to another consequence of not operationalizing these perspectives, which is that human beings are caught in a cycle of reacting to crises and fail to correct the root causes of the crises for long-term benefits. Applying these two perspectives develops shared consciousness for individuals and appreciation for how their actions affect their immediate environment as well as the global one, and other human beings, further activating their utu.

Maathai clarified that while the big- and long-view perspectives direct us toward effective far-reaching solutions and concrete practices, it is equally important to focus on the small perspective (Maathai 2010a, 67). In considering "the small," her call was not just for people to focus on their immediate environments in a general sense but also the individual parts that make up those ecosystems. It is necessary to consider the particularities and with that the interconnectedness of the parts of the small as well as of one small ecosystem to another. Maathai said, "It is also an infinitely subtle and intricate network of biomes that are full of microorganisms, bacteria, insects, plants, and other forms of life that are the bedrock of the larger ecosystems on which . . . more consumptive species such as our own depend" (68). She elaborated, saying, "Part of acknowledging the small and its connectedness is simply in noticing individual distress and the chain reaction it could stimulate" (69). Like the big picture, the small exists on different scales. A stream or pond is small in relation to the stretch of land on which it exists, which in turn is small in relation to the village. The village is small in relation to a district, which then scales up to a county, a country, and so on.

Seeing the big and small picture forces humans to become aware of the sources of things, which allows them to experience more of their humanness. Recognizing the sources of things provides an understanding of the interconnected needs and contributions of different components of ecosystems. Maathai, citing James Lovelock's Gaia hypothesis, promoted the idea of seeing the earth as one self-sustaining organism, with human beings as just one part of what makes up that organism (Maathai 2010a, 61–64). Being a part of an organism indicates that their true nature, humanness, is locked into how the rest of the body performs. Indeed, to disrespect or degrade the organism is to do the same to the self.

With the erasure of respect for the sources of things, human beings have constructed a false reality and belief in their absolute dominion over nature (Maathai 2010a, 71–73). Maathai shed light on how this misstep has compromised the capacity of human beings to appreciate their dependency on their environments and so interrupted their efforts to preserve those ecosystems. Underscoring human beings' vulnerability and dependency on the other parts of the organism that is the earth, she wrote, "It is a sobering thought that if the human species were to become extinct, no species I know of would die out because we were not there to sustain them. Yet if some of them became extinct, human beings would also die out. That should encourage us to have respect for the other forms of life and indeed for all of creation. We should demonstrate our gratitude for the way they sustain us" (2010a, 71). Recognizing this susceptibility humanizes the human in enhanced ways and also underlines human beings' communion and their reliance on each other and on nature, the essence of the philosophy of utu.

Applying these three perspectives, Maathai located human beings as occupying the summit as well as the base of the pyramid—in other words, as the ones most likely to influence trends of nature and maximize usage from their environments but also as the most vulnerable entities within their ecosystems. A close reading and analysis of this position reveals an unstated proposition that locates humans in relation to the need to protect the environment. She called for a continued quest for biological and other forms of knowledge about the environment (Maathai 2010a, 73–75), explaining that even science has barely cracked the surface of all there is to know about the environment. Clear in this position is not just a sense of wonder about the environment and a rationalization for further studies of the environment but also, more significantly, the lesson that it is too early to dismantle the environment or to reengineer it. If in fact human beings have a limited understanding of the environment, they cannot fully comprehend the ramifications of destroying it. Thus, it would be suicidal to destroy or reengineer the environment because there is no full understanding of it that would support its re-creation should the need arise. Additionally, failure to fully understand the environment and its ecosystems is hampering humans' understanding not just of their world but also of themselves and their capacities as part of that organism. Thus, as highest located and also most vulnerable, the human being does in fact have the greatest stake in seeing the environment protected and should bear the biggest burden in ensuring its defense.

In summary, Maathai suggested that human beings should be on a constant quest for knowledge about their environments in order to manage it justly and sustainably and also so they can fully access their own humanness. Meeting this task requires changes in attitudes and perspectives in time and space as well as thought. This should be reflected in how we relate to the environment, paying simultaneous attention to the longer view, the broader picture, and the small details and entities (Maathai 2010a, 67). She wrote, "The task for us in healing the Earth's wounds is to find a balance between the vertical and horizontal views; the big picture and the small; between knowledge based on measurement and data, and knowledge that draws on older forms of wisdom and experience" (76). The knowledge acquired through balancing multiple perspectives will inform the definition of holistic approaches.

To fully master this relationship to the environment requires contextualized analysis of the root causes of existing environmental conditions, which helps human beings learn from their pasts in designing futures. In the next section, I engage with Maathai's analysis of Kenya's environmental history to illustrate this idea. This history also offers further insight into how mismanaging the environment degrades humanity and humanness for both the destroyers and those affected by the destruction.

Denaturing the Environment: The Case of Kenya

For Maathai, environmental degradation and its effects on the continent of Africa were merely the symptoms of something more substantial, and so any real remedy required a consideration of the root causes. Growing into adulthood, she observed the depletion of the lush greenery and streams of her childhood days and later, as a scientist, understood this as a function of human interference (Maathai 2006). In response, Maathai promoted the idea of focusing on the triggers of disempowerment, poverty, lack of water, failing food security, poor health, and general letdowns, among other challenges (Maathai 2007a, 173; Maathai 2009b, 5). As part of this reflection, Maathai placed some responsibility at the feet of the citizens. Largely, however, she recognized that the environmental degradation was caused by external forces (Maathai 2007a, 173), observing that large-scale destruction of forests was not the work of the often-marginalized people who lived near them (Maathai 2010a, 38–55). The impoverished people who lived around forests, marginalized from control of the operations of modernity, were not the ones destroying forests (Maathai 2000, 41). They were just the ones most affected. Maathai pointed a finger at governments and companies as well as individuals such as poachers, conservationists, and tourists, many of them foreigners controlling and profiting from African lands and resources (Maathai 2009b, 229–33).

In Kenya, environmental degradation has affected rain cycles and agricultural and livestock production and caused a lack of basic day-to-day requirements such as food, firewood, and indigenous medicines for many. Kenyans experience consequences of this economically, politically and socially. In explaining why responsiveness to the root causes should inform approaches and philosophies of activism and critical thinking on the subject, Maathai distinguished an always-present connection of the human being to the land. She communicated the importance of sustaining that balance in her lecture "Bottlenecks to Development in Africa," drawing attention to indigenous African societies where food security was safeguarded at both the family and communal level and relating this to communities' day-to-day communion with their environments (Maathai 1995a). She spoke of the world of her childhood, where stabilized seasons and sustainable cultures of food production, processing, usage, storage, and distribution steadied food security and good health for not just the people but the physical environment as well. This picture is of an ecosystem in balance, with all the parts of the whole complementing and supporting each other, a reality that is necessary for the social, economic, and physical health and security of communities.

Having experienced this equilibrium, Maathai sought to pinpoint the source of environmental imbalances and related phenomena experienced in contemporary Kenya and indeed the rest of Africa (Maathai 2006). In an interview with Marianne Schnall (Maathai 2009d), she shared her journey, which began with rural women she encountered in her work. As she was confronted by their narratives expressing basic needs, including water, firewood, income, medicine, and food, she realized they were describing the failure of the environment to sustain them. Critically, she recognized these conditions as symptoms of larger systemic and structural root causes. Specifically, she traced their origins to the scourge of colonialism. Highlighting, like other decolonial thinkers, the impact of colonialism, racism, and capitalism, Maathai particularized the effects of this negative side of modernity to the question of the environment (Maathai 2009b, 233–34). To sustainably address the root causes of environment-attendant issues of underdevelopment, she argued, necessitated an interrogation of the exploitation perpetrated mostly by representatives of the Global North and their allies, spaces they plundered for profit and political control, and their culpability and responsibility (Maathai 1995a; *Taking Root* 2008). This was an exercise she undertook in relation to Kenya.

Out of the profit-obsessed colonial cosmos was born a culture of pillaging the environment without any concern for replenishing it. This happened through a deliberate process. To control the land, it was necessary for the colonialists to estrange the people from it. The capitalist and neoliberal ideologies and exercises of colonialism and, later, neocolonialism separated the people from the land, severing the communion that Maathai saw as essential to the survival of both. The expropriation of native land through the 1902 Crown Lands Ordinance stole from the people a personal stake in the land and erased their direct relationships to specific parcels of ancestral land. They became tenants on their own land, which was now owned by the Crown. Further erasure of ownership occurred when the 1915 Crown Lands Ordinance made possible ninety-nine-year leases for settlers (Onyango, Swallow, and Meinzen-Dick 2005, 5; Home 2012, 189–90). The institution of title deeds blatantly appropriated land from rightful owners, even erasing ancestral claims to it (Maathai 2010a, 227), and the creation of native reserves furthered this estrangement. As a consequence of colonialism and this alienation of colonial subjects from their land, a process of dehumanizing was actuated. Along with losing their land, they also experienced a reassignment of identities and ranks in this new societal order, what Maathai outlined as a form of eco-racism (Maathai 2007a).

As Africans lost their relationship to the land and their environment, their homes were destroyed, their land was appropriated, and forests they treasured for spiritual and other reasons were cut down to build residential native reserves (Maathai 2007a, 62; *Taking Root* 2008). In the reserves, created as a domicile for the displaced Africans, limited access to land and overpopulation resulted in a shortage of food and other resources (Kanyinga 2009, 327; Maathai 2007a, 67). At the same time, people were forced to migrate to find work for their survival, intensifying the disconnection from the land. The introduction of taxes forced native Kenyans to give up subsistence farming to seek wage labor. The human beings' relationship to the land was now redefined and corrupted by pressing financial needs and responsibilities. First, land was taken away. Second, the symbiotic relationship of care and use between the human and the land was obliterated. Third, the large numbers of people on small pieces of reserve land and departure from practices that had protected the land for centuries exhausted the land's productivity and quickly fatigued the soil. Fourth, the dehumanizing regulation of the movements of native Kenyans through the *kipande* identification system (Home 2012, 179) and the control of their labor affected how and where they worked the land (Kanyinga 2009, 328). The demands of colonialism transferred native Kenyans' time and labor from caring for their land, if they had any, to caring for someone else's land—the settlers'—in ways in which the settlers instructed. The new systems forced native Kenyans to farm foreign crop varieties and with methods foreign to their experience.

Maathai experienced this impact of colonialism personally. She grew up in a reality where white settlers who constituted less than 1 percent of the population controlled over 20 percent of Kenya's prime land, the so-called White Highlands. Hundreds of thousands of native Kenyans, including her family, were forced to live as squatters (Maathai 2007a, 62) and registered as resident native laborers, a system that KAU leaders called "new slavery." In this environment, the colonial-era introduction of a cash economy and cash-crop economies across Africa initiated threats to food security. The colonial administrators instructed against indigenous farming technologies and systems, representing them as inferior. Along with this were the introduction of monocultural plantations (Maathai 2010, 243–48) and the discarding of indigenous trees and crop cycles.

The colonialists' interests lay in maximizing profits from their colonies through exploiting agricultural production and other resources across the continent. The commercialization of agriculture through the introduction of cash crops inaugurated a food-purchasing culture as the centrality of indigenous crops was minimized. In various parts of the continent during and after colonialism, in order to survive by making enough money to buy the processed food the new realities forced them to consume, and in order to pay taxes, farmers committed what little productive land had been left under their control to cash crops. This was their way of asserting minimal financial agency in the new economy, which had locked out Africans. In Kenya, they planted crops such as coffee and tea, a practice that was detrimental to the soil (Maathai 2007a, 123). At the same time, indigenous trees fell victim to this profiteering scheme targeting natural resources (122). In the same way that cash crops replaced indigenous crops, fast-growing nonindigenous trees that were good for financial gain, including eucalyptus, black wattle, and conifers, began to replace indigenous forests. Maathai noted that for years this destabilization of indigenous ecosystems unleashed on the continent by some countries of the Global North had inhumanely privileged capitalism at the expense of the people's subsistence and survival—and their humanity (Maathai 2005b).

The introduction of such trees has been harmful on a number of levels. First, they could not match what the indigenous forests provided to meet the people's needs. The economics of trees (Maathai 2010a, 86–89), recognizing only the monetary value of trees, hindered people (even scientists) from considering the natural, social, psychological, and ecological services offered by the forests (86). The foreign trees also depleted local biodiversity and drained water resources (Maathai 2005b). These thirsty trees were draining water resources at the same time the land was being cleared of trees that would contribute to rain production to replenish that very reservoir of water the alien trees were exhausting. As an added consequence, indigenous crops that ensured food security were further jeopardized because they could not thrive without water. Even the cash crops introduced in attempts to financially maximize land productivity suffered. In some cases, there was simply an inadequate supply of water. When there was water, crops such as tea, which does not thrive in excessively wet conditions, were destroyed. Even more damning was the fact that loss of soil cover with the clearing of the land led to destructive erosion in parts and affected the production of crops, including those planted for subsistence (Maathai 2005b). Concurrently, manipulating natural environments affected rainfall patterns, which in turn disrupted the predictable planning and cycles of farming.

Along with these conditions, Eurocentric world senses and paradigms of colonialism encouraged the (mis)management of the environment. Eurocentric binary lenses of engaging the world generated hierarchies of bodies and entities, where white was better than black and human was better than nature. The humans could, therefore, manipulate and use their environment in any way that suited their interests. Maathai continually returned to African folktales to illustrate the fallacy of this way of thinking as well as the ills of depersonalizing human connections to natural resources. Such differentiation of entities in an environment breeds a lack of sensitivity to the interconnectedness of the various parts of that cosmos and its ecosystems. Through the colonial, Eurocentric lens, nature was viewed in terms of monetary potential. Trees, for example, simply became timber, and elephants were viewed as a source for ivory (*Taking Root* 2008). Having thus othered the environment, deference for the forces of nature dwindled and, with it, the people's utu. Maathai contended that African communities preserved forests because they realized the connectedness of their lives and humanity to that of the forest and they were not looking at natural resources and seeing money (*Taking Root* 2008).

These colonial disruptions effectively destroyed indigenous environmental cultures and heritages, which she was committed to restoring. This can be observed in her constant looking back into

Gikuyu cultural values and practices for solutions. These indigenous systems and practices, according to her, efficiently, sustainably, and equitably managed natural resources. Indeed, the GBM worked cultural knowledge into its seminars, and Maathai raised the question of culture being the missing link in some struggles with development on the continent (Maathai 2007a, 175). Eurocentric othering bent on convincing Africans of the inferiority of their environmental cultures helped tarnish indigenous ways of knowing and doing in common psyche and practice. Having succeeded, the colonizers and their allies were in a stronger position to steal the natural resources and redirect focus and perspectives, as was the case with the introduction of cash crops and the planting of trees that were unsustainable in the environment.

These maneuvers occasioned other systemic challenges. Two that Maathai examined were hunger and malnutrition. The idea of state food security introduced by the colonial administration erased traditional food-security systems and agency. This responsibility of the government to feed its people was transferred at independence to the new government, which, like the former colonial administration, failed to live up to the task (Maathai 1995a). Following independence and into the twenty-first century, governments continued to focus support toward cash crops, favored because they earned foreign funds through trade. The land, therefore, continued to fail the people. The effects of this were compounded by inadequate land (re)distribution by the government following independence and the displacement of some communities (Maathai 2009b, 228–29). The result has been denial of agency to people to produce food for their families, while at the same time the government has failed in its role of filling that gap in subsistence provision (Maathai 1995a).

Along with external forces, Maathai indicted postindependence governments for continuing practices that reproduced colonial propensities, and she placed responsibility for action at the feet of Africans. She suggested that it is damaging and self-sabotaging for Africans to continue to blame only colonialism for the issues faced with failed systems, institutions, and infrastructure (Maathai 2009b). A true battle, she offered, must be waged against "conflicts, warlordism, corruption, poverty, dependency and mismanagement in the region" (5). Submitting that there is enough responsibility to go around, she maintained that present-day global communities also have a role to play. At one point she strongly advocated for the attaching of conditions to foreign aid, in the form of African recipient countries applying a certain amount of their national resources toward sustainable environmental efforts. Even though she contended that such global initiatives must respect indigenous cultural heritage, it would be apposite to question whether or not this suggestion reproduces the very colonial gaze and control on African countries that she contested. It also counteracts her submission averring the "phenomenon of a national government being given directives by foreign envoys about national issues is also embarrassing because it is indicative of the amount of sovereignty African nations have already sacrificed so that they may be given aid and grants by the governments which such envoys represent" (Maathai 1995a).

The processes discussed in this section in many ways blighted the humanity and humanness of the colonizers and other profiteers as well as the native Kenyans. Therefore, the restorations of the environment and the institution of environmental justice occur hand in hand with a restoration of utu, especially for the oppressed. For Maathai, the pursuit of environmental restoration and justice is inseparable from that of utu, and this informed her brand of environmentalism, depicted and interpreted in the next sections.

Environmentalism as the Performance of Radical Utu

Holistic environmentalism as conceptualized by Maathai demands consciousness raising, self-empowerment, self-betterment, and a spirit of service and volunteerism (Maathai 2010a, 17). Her proposed interventions centered people as the actors and recipients of environmentalism using environmental justice as a path to economic, social, and political justice (14; Maathai 2009b, 240–43). These standards underpinned the core values and principles that emerge from the records of her life, words, and works to reveal what I have named radical utu—an indicator and driver of holistic environmentalism.

For Maathai, appropriate approaches for holistic environmental action began with the people—their needs, histories, capacities, spiritualities, geographies, and even their relationships (Maathai 2007a, 133). Because different people need different things from their environments and ecosystems, instituting holistic environmentalism demands a consideration of three principles that center both the people and their environment. First, any intervention must serve the people in a way that does not alienate them from their environment. Maintaining the people's connection to the land encourages continued knowledge acquisition about and from their physical world as well as respect for the environment. This inculcates a commitment to protecting the environment as well as an awareness of it and the sources that nourish it (138). Second, to ensure sustained service to the people, environmentalist approaches must focus on interrupting any further degeneration of the present ecosystems as well as restoring environments to their former glory. This notion of replenishing the earth, which became the title of one of Maathai's books, involves replacing what is taken out of the environment. She promoted the ideal of planting trees in place of any that are felled. Where foreign plants have ravaged ecosystems, replenishing would involve reintroducing the indigenous to restore the soil, water sources, and the ecosystems (Maathai 2010a, 74, 132). Maathai unceasingly highlighted the negative effects of disrupting ecosystems. She spoke often, for example, about the chain reaction caused by the introduction of foreign trees to central Kenya—water running downstream due to lost soil cover brings with it soil erosion, carrying the silt and soil to the lakes and seas to interrupt both human and animal dependence on these waterways (Maathai 2005b). Replenishing philosophies and practices rebuild and maintain cycles and circles of life and self-sustaining ecosystems.

Maathai deemed the third tenet, sustainability, a nonnegotiable ideal in designing interventions for holistic environmentalism. Achieving sustainability requires us to address the human factor in a number of ways. First, as noted above, is a focus on the needs of human beings, which requires a keen-sighted consideration of different demographics within their geographic, cultural, spiritual, social, economic, and political realities and ecosystems. Along with that, human beings have to be located as part of a wider natural ecosystem with a common destiny and evolution trajectory (Maathai 2010a, 194–95). Finally, solutions for holistic environmentalism must be people-driven, demanding the raising of individual and community eco-warriors who recognize their stake in the revolution to save their environments (Maathai 2000, 41).

Maathai led movements that modeled the philosophy of radical utu in environmentalism, advocating raising communities engaged with each other and their environments. This model can be applied to nurture leaders and eco-warriors in communities worldwide, ensuring sustainable resistance and environmental protection. For the model to work for specific communities, she emphasized the importance of first contextually understanding the complexity of the maladies. Such particularization can be observed in her study and intervention design for the situation in Kenya. Having historicized environmental degradation and its attendant ills as a function of the failures of the colonial and the modern African states (Maathai 2009b, 249), she contemplated how replenishing environments could combat the resulting economic, social, political, and cultural injustices on many levels. This informed the design of the GBM method.

It is from this big-picture perspective that Maathai defined environmental protection and replenishing as political action, referring, for example, to the GBM tree planting as a "symbol of our defiance" (2006). She demonstrated how tree planting could be viewed as both a disrupter and a strong peace-building tool. She said, "Ordinarily no one should be bothered about a bunch of women trying to plant a tree" (2006), implying that it was what else the GBM family championed that was threatening. In the following, I probe expansions to this concept of environmental protection as civil disobedience to highlight the revolutionary and radical nature of people-driven environmentalism.

Conceding the political, economic, cultural, and social value of the environment and how individuals can deploy environmental spaces and action to negotiate and bargain authority and power underlines environmental action's political facility. Tree planting and environmental protection is, in this way, conceptualized as a political process that can establish or restore security and balance. Civil disobedience was a part of the Wangari Maathai brand. Vertistine Mbaya, Maathai's close friend and confidant, notes that Maathai was disobedient at a time when it was not acceptable to be disobedient (*Taking Root* 2008)—during Moi's presidency. This noncompliance spurred running battles between her and her partners on the one hand and representatives of the government of Kenya on the other during the 1980s and 1990s. It is therefore no surprise that a close study of her writings, speeches, and activist engagements reveals ideas that make the case for conceptualizing environmental activism as radical political action. The following statement captures this: "Just as invading forces know that cutting down sacred groves and trees can assist in quelling a community's recalcitrance, so resistance to the imposition of different social or religious customs, or economic agendas, has sometimes taken the form of communities rallying to protect trees" (Maathai 2010a, 97). In what ways, then, can environmental conservationism manifest as radical political engagement?

Combating the depletion of natural resources and saving indigenous plant life must be viewed as direct political action that challenges the ills and legacies of colonialism and Eurocentrism. It also stands as political action against the bad governance of modern states. Maathai noted that for development to be present, human needs had to be met through fair and sustainable management and distribution of resources. She made connections between the loss of security and human rights, dictatorial rule, and exploitation by outside forces primarily from the Global North. She used the Cold War to demonstrate this, suggesting that it had created an environment where political and economic tyranny accompanied by human rights violations were acceptable. In this reality, any contestation by citizenry was quelled summarily and often inhumanely (Maathai 1995a; 2009b, 33). She suggested that the false exhibition of progress, safety, and peace supported and covered up the continued brutalizing of natural environments and citizens and fed civil wars in some African countries, including Sudan, Ethiopia, Somalia, Angola, Mozambique, and Liberia. Key to her postulations was the fact that this misinformation about free progress in Africa was a necessary part of the Cold War. It was an excuse to arm and militarize African spaces and create a market for goods, including weapons, as well as ideas and ideologies from the superpowers and their allies, while concomitantly creating conditions perfect for draining Africa's natural resources. In Maathai's words, "the Cold War was not cold in Africa" (1995a). Viewed through this lens, contesting political and economic coercion through environmental replenishment that relocates agency to affected communities and societies as well as ownership and control of their environments is clearly political action.

The politics of food is another environmentally influenced subject that epitomizes this theory. Maathai noted that food had become a political weapon controlled by those in power (Maathai 2010a, 2009b, 1995a). For agriculturally dependent countries, the effects could even be felt at state level. The issues are more significant among those dependent on production of food for subsistence as well as economic development, as is the case in many African nations. If food is a political tool, then independent, people-driven food production campaigns equate to civil revolution as a path to liberation. In

Kenya, for example, Maathai and the GBM sought to relocate the power of producing food to the hands of local communities (Maathai 2009b, 2005b, 2003). This was a response to national policies related to agriculture continuing the colonial practices that discouraged or estranged local farmers from food production. The national policies promoted imported, less-healthy processed foods and cash-crop production. Food production revolutions further allow the people to defy poverty and poor health, impacting livelihood and productivity as well as their capacity to participate in other ways politically. Maathai urged citizens to plant and consume indigenous food crops that flourished in their environments, which had the added benefit of replenishing indigenous biodiversity (1995a). On the same subject of food politics, she waded into controversial waters as a strong opponent of the introduction of genetically modified crops to African environments (2005c, 38). In this instance, she used this standpoint to contest economic oppression of Africans by the Global North, as covered in chapter 5.

Others have acknowledged the political capacity of environmentalism as conceptualized by Wangari Maathai. Her work, which suggested societal and political conflict—a manifestation of degradation of utu—were inextricably related to natural resources management and distribution, led the Norwegian Nobel Committee, for the first time in history, to acknowledge the correlations between natural resources protection, human rights, and peace. Maathai linked the breakout of conflicts across Africa and the world to environmental degradation and the competition for resources (Mazur and Louella 2009, 224; Maathai 2006). In announcing the award, the committee stated, "Peace on earth depends on our ability to secure our living environment. Maathai stands at the front of the fight to promote ecologically viable social, economic and cultural development in Kenya and in Africa. She has taken a holistic approach to sustainable development that embraces democracy, human rights and women's rights in particular. She thinks globally and acts locally" (Norwegian Nobel Committee 2004). In her acceptance speech, Maathai stated that "the Norwegian Nobel Committee has placed the critical issue of environment and its linkage to democracy and peace before the world" (2004c). It is with this awareness that Maathai defined environmental conservation as political work, as a symbol of defiance, and defined what I have named utu-driven eco-revolution. In the next section, I outline the anatomy of this type of revolution.

Utu-Driven Eco-revolution

This model of ecological revolution is facilitated by a number of principles, all observable in Maathai's activism. The first is that environmental movements and campaigns are allied to, inspire, and are inspired by other revolutions. Tree planting, something almost everyone can do, has the potential to spark participation and ownership by many and serve as a path to other revolutions. Planting trees therefore becomes an end in itself and at the same time a path to other revolutionary spaces and ideals. Maathai noted that "a tree for us is a symbol, it's an entry point, and once you are into the communities then you help the communities to try and understand the linkages and to try to mobilize them for action" (2009d). For the communities of the GBM, for example, one must contemplate the relations between their conditions and needs, their environments, and the state (Maathai 2009b, 227–38). Once their primary needs had been met, they could actively participate in democratic and socioeconomic activities. Solving the women's and communities' immediate problems through production of wood fuel, fencing, and building materials and replenishing forests, ground cover, and water-catchment areas opened doors for the community members' participation as citizens in other arenas. They demanded policy changes and put in place structures to combat malnutrition and hunger, improve their low economic status, and heighten their political participation (Maathai 2007a, 180–82). They could also manage their families' physical health as well as spiritual and emotional health through practices such as fighting for the protection of open green spaces, especially in urban centers (173–74). The ecological revolution she modeled created opportunities for mass participation of citizens and communities in the management of resources while holding governments accountable to facilitate proper eco-friendly governance and other democratic spaces.

Another principle of utu-driven revolutions is that they go from the particular to the general. The GBM approach focused on resolving issues specific to communities (Maathai 2007a, 123–25; 2000, 41). The result of this methodology is a restoration and stabilization of contextualized ecosystems, which returns power to the people taking charge of their immediate environment. A multiplication of this effect can create a global community of eco-warriors. As they participate in the same movement globally, a sense of *communitas* is established, and a shared humanity and humanness is experienced.

The third principle conceptualizes environmental movements as people's revolutions. Maathai imagined movements for green recovery designed as ones that most citizens of the world can create and participate in at different levels. In her words, "planting a tree is a very doable thing. It's not complicated, it doesn't require technology, it doesn't require much knowledge" (2009d). She furthered this principle beyond trees to general environmental protection by invoking the global three Rs of the environment—reuse, reduce, recycle—to highlight the capacity for all-inclusiveness even at individual level across cultures, classes, literacy levels, and geographic locations (Maathai 2007a, 138; 2006; 2009d). In a 2004 interview on National Public Radio, Maathai illustrated the uncomplicated nature of this kind of revolution and its inclusivity, stating, "There's a lot we can do with our own hands, and don't need technology, and do not much need support from the government. Just mobilizing our physical energies" (Maathai 2004a). Meeting individual responsibility generates collective achievement. Underlining the potential impact of replicating small individual efforts a few million times, she later shared the well-known narrative of the hummingbird (Maathai 2009d). Maathai also advocated accentuating individuals' contributions because "none of us is that useless that we cannot improve the environment in which we live" (Duke 2004).

The fourth principle relates directly to the previous one. She abstracted the capacity of green movements to succeed as guerrilla-style uprisings. Being people-driven revolutions locates them as launched against hegemonic societal, business, and political systems and interests. She articulated a bottom-up approach as key to the success of a global environmental conservation movement, contending that trickle-down approaches did not serve the poor (Maathai 1995a). Such an ideal allows for personalization and so ownership of the movement by different groups of protesting individuals globally. For each collective or community, this approach makes the most of relevant "creative energies, expertise, knowledge and capabilities of local" people (1995a). Applying the particular energies, abilities, creativities, and proficiencies of the people in a community maximizes benefits from such capacities and amplifies them, as their use offers opportunities for honing these skills and facilities. It therefore promotes the development of human and other resources and competencies unimpeded by illiteracy or low levels of formal education (1995a).

A guerrilla approach that empowers the people creates local or global communities with a clear stake and investment, which are then better placed to demand accountability from their governments. While encouraging a bottom-up approach, Maathai highlighted the role of governments and businesses (Maathai 2009b, 15–18, 23–24, 268–73) in this process of change making. She posited that empowered citizens could demand that governments work with them (2009d), with such a relationship balancing the responsibilities of citizens and governments. Projecting citizen action that holds governments accountable, she resolved, "only strong, informed nonstate actors of the civil society would persuade its government not to sacrifice the local farmers at the altar of international food politics and profiteering" (Maathai 1995a). Maathai also outlined the responsibilities of businesses calling for green technologies and green jobs but argued that the responsibility for taking a longer view in the use and management of resources should not be left to businesses (Mazur and Louella 2009, 218; Maathai 2009b, 14). She charged that the masses should retain the power and duty of holding businesses accountable (Mazur and Louella, 219). Whether governments and others do their part or not, the people's obligation remains, which they can meet through votes or direct action, literally or figuratively getting their hands dirty (Maathai 2007a, 173). The need for self-driven eco-warriors is even more pressing with today's struggles against government and business representatives who are climate-change deniers.

What Maathai helped define, and what the Nobel Prize committee celebrated, is a model for peaceful, radical, human-driven ecological revolutions. Her ideals and ideas evidence the interactions between ecological concerns and human and civil rights as exhibited in two highly publicized efforts: the campaigns to save Karura Forest and Uhuru Park. Both campaigns, demonstrations of utu-driven eco-revolution, challenged development plans that disregarded environmental protection at a time when Kenya's population had grown from eight million at independence to about twenty-eight million and natural resources to sustain the population were dwindling. The narrative of Karura Forest, positioning Maathai and her partners and supporters as utu-driven eco-warriors, is presented in appendix 2. The Karura Forest struggle employed ecological revolution techniques as civil disobedience.

The fight to save Uhuru Park by protesting the erection of the Times Media Trust Complex, examined in chapter 4, offers another illustration of this model of eco-revolution. In that particular crusade, in February 1992, government agents finally cleared out of the proposed building site for the project at the park. Maathai led women leaders in an impromptu march to the location, where she placed a wreath to celebrate the death of the project. While this was a struggle about saving green spaces, it was also primarily one against corruption, land grabbing, and impunity of leaders. Indeed, the Times Media Trust Complex confrontation, which resulted in the GBM's eviction from government offices, prompted increased government hostility toward the GBM and Maathai. As a result, she spent 1990 and 1991 settling GBM employees into her home, which would become the GBM's base for a number of years—another example of the importance of the people's ownership of any successful revolution.

In engaging environmentalism, Maathai looked at both natural ecosystems and human-made political, social, cultural, and economic ecosystems. Her work made associations between corrupt, dehumanizing colonial and postindependence governance and poor management of natural resources and the emotional, mental, economic, social, and physical well-being of the citizenry. Her holistic environmentalism, outlined in this chapter, covers these intersecting concerns. This conceptualization recognizes that healthy citizens, provided for by a healthy self-sustaining environment, can more actively and independently participate in dynamic sustainable development. Using the trial-and-error approach and training platforms such as seminars and workshops (Maathai 2010a; 2003), Maathai educated communities on the connections between environmental degradation and the challenges to the lives and livelihoods of individuals and communities. The primary lesson was that environmental degradation happens in tandem with the degradation of humanness and humanity. To wit, environmental degradation effects dehumanization of the people just as the loss of utu in people effects abuse of the environment.

3

Eco-agency and Unbowed Personhood

A Decolonial Imagining of Equity

A narrow profiling that focalizes only Wangari Maathai's activism with grassroots Kenyan women has effectively undermined the recognition of her global impact on women's rights and liberation and her contributions to regional and global women's movements. As a result, scholars and activists often fail to recognize the potential of her ideas and ideals to inform critical and decolonial women's and human rights studies and praxis. I seek to underline Maathai's often forgotten position as a leading critical thinker of women's and gender studies and activism. It is important to note that as the postindependence Kenyan and African women's movements and the global women's movement were pullulating, Maathai's social position, training, and growing international profile gave her a perspective that tenders credibility to critical ideas and ideals she developed or espoused on women's liberation.

Maathai's return to Nairobi from the United States and later Germany launched her public life as a supporter of her husband's political ambitions at the very time she was defining a professional one as a professor and a private one as a wife and mother (Maathai 2007a, 109–11; 1994, 8). These private and public identities came of age within a short time period, creating a unique advocate for women's rights. Local and global developments and initiatives historicized in chapter 1 primed Maathai's identity as a champion for women's rights at a time when her location in the political landscape during her husband's tenure in parliament brought her in direct contact with grassroots women, and she entered two other worlds—the academic arena and the fast-growing postindependence national and continental women's movements. In discussing Maathai's achievements, little attention has been paid to this privileged economic, social, and political position she occupied in the 1970s, the point in history when her journey as a public champion for women's rights began.

As a well-traveled politician's wife and the woman with the highest level of formal education in East and Central Africa, Maathai was well positioned to not only access information on local and global issues and initiatives relevant to the women's rights struggle but also strategically participate in these domestic and global political and social developments. She could view the happenings of the time and women's experiences, politics, and movements through the eyes of marginalized developing-world populations as well as the privileged position of an elite scholar and activist with a global outlook. Her academic training provided tools with which she critically and analytically processed this information and the issues of the times. Her activism and grassroots work, therefore, enlightened and complemented by her academic profile, experience, and expertise, were marked by clear critical philosophies and theories. This allowed her to articulate academic and activist positions and critical thoughts that we can draw from or apply to define a decolonial approach to women's empowerment, which I tease out in this chapter.

Maathai's public exertions toward the empowerment of women began in earnest in the early seventies, a time when Kenya's social, political, and economic national spaces appeared relatively peaceful. Several realities, including single-party politics and the absence of a significant collective voice of the citizenry to highlight struggles for resources, along with healthy daily servings of the nationalizing and Kenyanizing *harambee* ideology,[1] furnished the impression of an inclusive national ethos with ethnic and other differences kept below the surface. Succession politics and the failed coup of 1972 are examples of masked conflicts finding their way in snatches to the surface. This facade of a new Kenya for all Kenyans was tainted by the fact that efforts to nationalize and Kenyanize had not resolved questions related to the place of women in the national economy or public social and political spaces. Women as equal citizens and people were not favorably considered in the constitution of this new patriarchal national space nor were their contributions to their people's histories, economies, politics, and cultures (Muhonja 2016). Maathai's position gave her access to such information as well as tools and networks that could support her critical responses to these challenges for women in the budding nation and beyond.

Maathai espoused liberation efforts for women grounded in and contextualized to specific realities, cultures, and histories—in effect a decolonization of women's liberation initiatives. In relation to African women, she opined that the values and strategies for such processes toward empowerment would have to consider indigenous ways of being and knowing, echoing the words of Fikret Berkes and Mina Kislalioglu Berkes: "Holism is the key characteristic of indigenous knowledge" (2009, 8). Maathai's ideals and ideas on women's rights emphasized holistic interactions and cross influences between people, their cultural values and practices, and environments. Her approach sought to empower women through delivering agency to act and influence the realities of their natural and human-made social and physical environments. This is exemplified in the way she processed the primary needs and the solutions to challenges faced by grassroots women in Kenya. Per her evaluation, harmony and balance between nature and people had been ensured by indigenous African ways of knowing and being. Failure to sustain that knowledge, and with it the complementary relationship between human and environment, had compromised the location of women in society in relation to their autonomy and capacity to provide for their families. This assessment informed, to a large extent, the design of her principles and campaigns for women's rights, as illustrated in the following account.

The formation of the GBM, Maathai's primary channel for her activities on women's rights, was inspired by her observation that "women from rural areas and urban centers, reflecting on their needs at organized forums, spoke about environmental degradation. They did not have firewood. They needed fruits to cure malnutrition in their children" (Kennedy and Richardson 2004, 38). Maathai contrasted this with her experiences and those of her mother with their social and natural environment. In various interviews she reflected on her own upbringing and the capacity of mothers to relate to and harness their environment to provide for families, saying, "When I was a child, I would go to the river, and fetch water for my mother. I would come home. We would drink it. We didn't even boil it. . . . As a child, I was collecting firewood for my mother in the wood lots" (2006). This provision of nature, for women, was accompanied by culturally assured agency to control those resources, as Maathai narrates, "for my mother." These conditions of the well-functioning ecosystem consisting of social and physical environments sustaining humans and vice versa were starkly different from the imbalance experienced by the grassroots women Maathai worked with. It was the restoration of such a natural and cultural ecosystem that she sought as a pathway to women's empowerment.

Maathai offered a different reading on the gendering of social, economic, and political privilege, constructing new paths to rebalancing power in societies. I outline her holistic philosophy of women's empowerment as rooted in three ideals: it is human-rights focused, decolonial, and eco-directed. Her position was that celebrating and mastering their multilayered natures and relationships to their physical, cultural, and social environments allows women to deploy these natures and relationships toward autonomy and rebalancing societal power. This kind of comprehension of the self in relation to one's environments, which admits people into spaces and roles where they impact societal rebalancing, must pivot on conceptualizations of women and womanhood from within specific indigenous cultures. As modeled by Maathai, for Kenyan and other African women, this ideological approach has to be effectually grounded by unapologetic Africanness and departure from Western characterizations of African identities and societal practices.

She situated this decolonial African responsiveness to rebalancing society as entrenched in utu. The definition of utu that this chapter references denotes personhood. Desmond Tutu offers cognition of personhood as multidirectional. His explanation asserts that to claim humanity, one must equally concede and honor the personhood of all other persons, recognizing that their own personhood is dependent on that of every other person. He states, "In our culture, there is no such thing as a solitary individual. We say, 'A person is a person through other persons.' That we belong in the bundle of life. And I want you to be all you can be because that's the only way I can be all I can be. . . . I need you to be you so that I can be me. And that's why we say, when you dehumanize another, whether you like it or not, inexorably you are yourself dehumanized" (Tutu 2007). Applying this filter engenders respect for all *watu* and utu—persons and personhoods, recognizing women first as equal humans before highlighting their womanhood. This way of being and knowing esteems women's identities and bodies, the capacities and power imbued in both, as well as their knowledge—the very definition of empowerment and liberation.

Human, Not Woman

Maathai's focus on people rather than women may be why she appeared to prefer using the expression "human rights" to "feminism." She did not see the rights of women as isolatable from those of the rest of society. Her approaches to ensuring societal equity, therefore, focused on being human and not being woman. Maathai rarely located women as "other" to men. She debated women's needs, challenges, and empowerment without presenting them in opposition to male spaces. In so doing, she defined female identities that are not patricentric or defined by patriarchy and whose value does not require affirmation against a masculine other. Because she did not read women's authority and autonomy through a gendered lens, she contested gendered constructions and expectations on her person and identity, asserting, "I had never thought of myself as an African woman. I had never thought of myself as a woman. . . . For me the limit was my capacity, my capability" (*Taking Root* 2008).

Her actions grounded in such contestation prompted calls by some critics, including Kenya's then-president Moi and other government officials, for her to perform her womanhood in acceptable ways. Moi and his cohort directed other women to "manage" Maathai, who was stepping out of line "as a woman." In one nationally televised speech, the president called on women to "discipline" Maathai, who was transgressing societal rules by not acting like a woman and not showing the requisite "respect" to men. This continued verbal assault on women, including Maathai, accompanied by threats, led to a reaction from women leaders and a news story on October 10, 1991, in the *Daily Nation* titled "Watch Your Words! Women Tell Politicians!"

As Maathai's global responsibilities and profile grew, so did these detractors' efforts to discredit her. In one occurrence, both Moi and Maathai attended the 1992 United Nations Conference on Environment and Development known as the Earth Summit in Rio de Janeiro, where she participated in a press conference alongside US senator Al Gore and the Dalai Lama. She reported that at the summit the Kenyan government, using workers of state-owned media, sponsored a campaign to malign her as a bad influence on women and not deserving of this global platform (Maathai 2007a, 228). Even with the reported government antics to malign her, the international nongovernmental organizations collective selected Maathai to serve as its spokesperson at the summit. She would go on to present women's views for the five-year review of the so-called Earth Summit at special sessions of the UN General Assembly. Significant to note from this is the fact that, in her disparagers' judgment, she was "causing" other women to act as "not women"—in effect jettisoning their "proper" and acceptable womanhood in accordance with patriarchal constructions.

This reluctance of Maathai's to privilege gender is captured in her response to an MP who, as a way of putting her in her place "as a woman," threatened to "circumcise" her if she ever visited Rift Valley Province. Her rejoinder to this was "I'm sick and tired of men who are so incompetent that every time they feel the heat because women are challenging them, they have to check their genitalia to reassure themselves. I'm not interested in that part of the anatomy." She added, "The issues I'm dealing with require the utilization of what's above the neck. If you don't have anything there, leave me alone" (Mbaria 2004). This figuration erases focus on body parts below the neck where biology may indicate differences. By focusing on the region above the neck where there are mostly similarities, Maathai presents herself and other women as people, not women or men, and forces an erasure of feminizing women as a public standard. Additionally, she highlights the equal intellectual capacity of women and men.

This propensity to erase society's tendency to gender certain entities is also observable in her representations of her family. While not eroding her father's significance in their lives, for example, Maathai habitually referenced the family holdings in Ihithe as her mother's property without invoking the place of her father. It was her mother who first ceded to her a small plot of land to cultivate as her own and nurtured her love for the land (Maathai 2007a, 38). Maathai clarified that this was not a practice unique to her mother but rather a value of Gikuyu societies (4). In the powerful imagery provided in the narration of what would have been her first day in the world, she depicts a collective of female members of society supporting her introduction to the world with the natural produce from their farms, cementing the fact that not as a woman but as a human being of the Gikuyu community she is inextricably linked to the land.

Maathai's work with the GBM equally focalized female members of society as individuals and collectives managing their physical environments and their homes but did so without locating the GBM as an exclusively women's movement. She presented the movement as inclusive, stating in an interview with Marianne Schnall of the *Huffington Post* in 2009, "We also learned that very quickly the men realized that planting trees, yes indeed, it is a very good way of improving the quality of the land, and the value of the land. So many of the men eventually joined in, and also the children joined in" (2009a). Men appreciated the value of the work and joined the movement (Kennedy and Richardson 2004; Maathai 2007a, 175). She went on: "The Green Belt Movement enjoys the participation of men, women, and children, which is important. You could very easily have the women planting trees and the men cutting the trees down! Everyone needs to work together and to protect the environment together" (Kennedy and Richardson 2004). As with her family's story, while the GBM concentrated from the outset on women, it did not seek to explain the absence of men or position the women in a struggle against men. Rather, the challenges for the women were defined as against colonial impact, systemic failures in governance, and poor land and resource management. She did not offer any scenarios where there was a need to coerce or seek the specific gendered approval of men in establishing the GBM and its networks, in the use of public land, or even in agreements about what their wives were doing, for those who had husbands. She reported disruptions only as experiences with individual men, such as certain politicians, members of law enforcement, and foresters, and not men in general or the men directly connected to the resources these women were tapping and developing.

I complete this section with a quote that highlights the utu, personhood—not *uke*, femininity or womanhood—quality of Maathai's approach to the rights of women: "We are dealing with the rights of the public and the rights of the people. These are the kind of issues that require the anatomy of whatever lies above the neck" (2000). Such a response to the human and not the woman, in many Kenyan cultures, was preserved by the philosophy of utu, humanness, and a respect for utu, personhood. It is this that allowed female members of society access to means of protest that activists, scholars, and others can deploy in the present day to reestablish a balance where women's equal personhood is recognized, examples of which I present in the next section. It is important to note that in indigenous African societies such power was not enjoyed by women because they were women but because they held and occupied certain identities and roles, which were revered.

Identities and Bodies as Political Tools

It was a great ceremony to see those young men come out of
jail and also to celebrate the powers of their mothers.

—Wangari Maathai (2000)

Indigenous ways of knowing and being in many African and Kenyan
cultures imbue certain bodies and identities with unique social, spiritual, and political power and influence. Some of these bodies and
identities present as anatomically female, and their occupiers often in-
voke these bodies and identities in protest. Activating bodies as tools
for resistance can be revolutionary and disruptive to contemporary
world mentalities, which tend to police and regulate female bodies
and demand of them certain aesthetic and performance standards
(Barake-Yusuf 2009, Dlova et al. 2014, Nchimbi 2005, Mougoué
2016). Women's bodies acting outside of these expectations are then
judged or shamed. In many indigenous African cultures, certain disrupting and "unruly" female bodies are protected by cultural mores.
This ensures that such "unruliness" elevates rather than degrades
the bodies, safeguarding respect for words and actions articulated by
the bodies. I use, in the following, two landmark happenings from
Maathai's life that capture the idea of an agential body in political
protest to demonstrate this application of some female identities and
bodies as tools for protest.

Both events channel indigenous practices common to many African cultures. The first, the act of "sitting," is the equivalent of the
modern-day sit-in combined with protest by obstruction. The second
involves the use of a revered body to defy unwanted action. I note
as I present these two events that the promotion of the female body
as a political tool was repeatedly epitomized in Maathai's activism
through assaults on her body. The intention is not to glorify abuse
of the female body. What is important for this analysis is recognition
of the visual representation of that body in struggle and in civil disobedience that bore desired results. Also important to note is the fact
that while some of the outrage expressed by the public and supporters was because the assault was against a female member of society,
Maathai never presented herself as helpless in these circumstances
or suggested that she was fighting "as a woman." She was in battle
as a human being and sometimes as a Kenyan. After being violently
attacked in the Karura Forest, she declared, "If we are going to shed

blood because of our land, we will! We are used to that. Our fore-
fathers shed blood for our land. We will do so. This is my blood, and it
reminds me of the blood that Waiyaki[2] shed trying to protect Karura
Forest" (*Taking Root* 2008). Maathai also often presented herself and
her body as one in service in a uniquely empowering way (*Taking Root*
2008). In so doing, she offered a new view of the concept "service" and
bodies in service, defining the concept of empowered service (Maathai
2010a, 115; Maathai 2006). It is this ideal that she instilled in the
women of the GBM. What she promoted was not blind sacrificial
service. She advocated, first, service to self, arguing that the action
of centering oneself in processes of serving the community dictates
agency and reimagines the idea of oppression and coercion of female
bodies. In a 2000 essay on women and the environment, she states,
"You have every right to read what you want to read. You want to
meet—without asking permission. To get off the bus means to control the direction of your own life" (Maathai 2000). Second, in the
statement following the one cited here and elsewhere, she emphasized
that, in service, centering of the self must be accompanied by a control of resources. This constitutes agency.

The first illustrative event of the application of bodies as political
tools was an incident on January 10, 1992, that set in motion a chain
of events that landed Maathai in another public confrontation with
Moi and his government. Through a succession of episodes, her body,
locked in protest, was both besieged and threatened. She "imprisoned"
herself not only to avoid arrest but as a statement—a sit-in, protest
by obstruction, and standoff that caught the attention and rallied the
support of people across the world. That body, which was then jailed
and judged, served as a symbol for resistance and freedom.

On the day in question, Maathai and others reported receiving a
call during a meeting at the Ngong Hills Hotel in Nairobi of FORD,
the party and coalition against one-party rule in Kenya. The caller
had information that Maathai and others were on a list of opposition
leaders targeted for assassination and that President Moi planned to
sponsor a coup against democratic institutions that would hand power
over to the military, which he controlled. Ten prodemocracy leaders,
including Maathai, Paul Muite, and James Orengo, immediately held
a preemptive press conference at the Chester House office building,
which was at the time a hub for international media organizations
and journalists in downtown Nairobi. Their goal was to ensure their
safety and that of the nation in the event that the rumors were true.

They warned against any planned hijacking of the country, counseling Moi to wait for proper elections. The response from the government was swift: orders to arrest the ten.

Maathai barricaded herself in her house. In the three-day siege and standoff that followed, her local and international supporters and members of the press held vigil outside her compound, communicating with her via phone while police stood watch. On the first day, the police managed to get past the gate but not into her house, which had structural security reinforcements. Her phone service was eventually disconnected on government orders directed at isolating her. On the third day, government forces used tools to cut through the locks and bars of her windows and doors and arrested her on charges of sedition, treason, and spreading malicious rumors. One news report read, "After more than 100 police barricaded her house over the weekend, police broke in Monday afternoon and pulled her through a window" ("Wangari Maathai Arrested" 1991). Public and international outcry over her arrest was intense. The story was covered by CNN on the program *Future Watch* and by *Time* magazine, among other outlets. Maathai had won the Goldman Environmental Award that year, and the Goldman Foundation mobilized twenty-three directors of environmental organizations across the world to sign a letter protesting her arrest ("Wangari Maathai Arrested" 1991).

Maathai was kept in a bare, cold, wet cell, with lights left on around the clock, leaving her cripplingly ill from arthritic inflammation, lack of sleep, and extreme hunger. She reported that as she was carried to court to answer to the charges because, in her pain and exhaustion, she was incapable of walking, she focused her gaze on a group of women bearing a banner that read, "Wangari, Brave Daughter of Kenya, You Will Never Walk Alone Again" (Maathai 2007a, 215). After she received bail, the intervention of global communities, including members of the US Senate Committee on Foreign Relations, resulted in the charges against her and her codefendants being dropped by November 1992. The publicly displayed imagery of her body under siege and in a standoff with government powers, then dehumanized by them, and finally "unbowed" and triumphing to fight another day, stands as a symbol of oppression—and also resistance and liberation.

The second event I reference demonstrates the power carried in a particular identity. Recognizing the clout of certain female identities, in this case that of mother, Maathai advocated for mother-centered considerations for women's empowerment. It is not necessary to recap here what other scholars have said on the question of African motherhood and power (wa Tushabe 2014; Pala 2013; Nzegwu 2009, 2006, 2004; Sudarkasa 2004; Oyewumi 2015, 2003, 1997; Amadiume 1997; Muhonja 2013; Mutongi 1999). I note here simply that Maathai's ideas aligned with those of the cited scholars, including Ifi Amadiume. Amadiume captures this aptly in *Re-inventing Africa: Matriarchy, Religion, and Culture:* "The traditional power of African women had an economic and ideological basis, and derived from the sacred and almost divine importance accorded to motherhood. This has led me to argue that the issue of the structural status of motherhood is the main difference between the historical experiences of African women and those of European women" (1997, 146). Like these scholars, Maathai located motherhood as multidimensional and multilayered. She signified, in her writing, collective motherhood (Maathai 2007a, 4–5, 18), earth motherhood (4), lineage motherhood (5), generational motherhood (13), othermotherhood (18), social motherhood (4, 13, 18), and spiritual motherhood (Maathai 2010a, 21, 30).

Maathai saw the agency and power permeating the mother identity as valuable to the struggle for social justice for women and societies. The application of this is observable in her deliberations on the GBM's identifying and resolving the challenges of grassroots women. Regarding the connection between the GBM's methods and women's empowerment, she noted that women were the first victims of environmental degradation because it affected their capacity to provide water, fuel, and food, among other needs for their families (Maathai 2009d; Kennedy and Richardson 2004, 38). The women she worked to assist had lost the capacity to leverage the environment to provide for children on basic and emotional need levels. When they could access the food, it failed to sufficiently protect their children from disease or offer adequate energy (38). Thus, for many of the grassroots women she encountered through the years, under pressure to provide basic needs for their families, their immediate anxieties were rooted to a large extent in their responsibilities as mothers, their mothering, and motherwork.

This simple insight illuminates connections between the challenges experienced by the human mother and the solution—Mother Earth. The protective and productive relationship between the two is symbiotic. Maathai's own narrative speaks of her entry into a world celebrating maternal capacity to sufficiently provide for children from the bounty of Mother Earth. She relates, "When a baby joined the community, a beautiful and practical ritual followed that introduced the infant to the land of the ancestors, and conserved a world of plenty and good that came from that soil" (2007a, 4). She shares the Gikuyu community's practice in which, upon the birth of a child, othermothers brought to the birth mother green bananas, sweet potatoes, and purple sugarcane. To complement this bold harvest that connects the work and bounty of Mother Earth and that of human mothers was a lamb (4). The new mother chewed the roasted bananas, potatoes, lamb meat, and raw sugarcane, each in turn. She would then feed some of the juice from that effort to the baby as the baby's first meal. Per Maathai's analysis, shared later in the chapter, the initial establishing of all human beings' connection at birth to the land among the Gikuyu was a practice managed by women performing as mothers.

With the narrative of her mother and othermothers, Maathai placed earth motherhood and human motherhood at the center of life and survival, of the wholeness and wellness of society. Further, in highlighting the collective passing on of these connections to the child, she presented the mother as guardian of that relationship between nature and human and as transmitter of that power through generations. Mother Earth protects the human being if the human being protects Mother Earth (Maathai 2004c). Maathai further articulated how indigenous technologies and knowledges of mothers and motherhood, some of which they used to sustainably manage and tap the environment for food, medicine, fuel, spirituality, and other basics, can afford empowerment and reclamation of mother power (Maathai 2007a, 5, 11, 136). It is this empowered mother body, irreplaceably located as sacred codeliverer of life—as the only vessel through which human life enters the world—that also gives it its capacity to influence change.

The performance of the mother body in many indigenous Kenyan communities as a tool and conduit for change remains acknowledged and was manifest in the case of the Release Political Prisoners campaign. It was while in hospital recuperating from the effects of her 1992 detention that Maathai's next cause was brought to her bedside by Koigi Wamwere's mother, Monica Wamwere, representing mothers of political prisoners who with others operated as the RPP lobbying group. Empowered by the women's movement and the new political climate following the December 1991 repeal of section 2A of Kenya's constitution, they had chosen to fight for the release of their children. Their position was that with the new changes to the constitution, the government had no reason to hold their sons, whose arrest was illegal in the new multiparty era. Upon leaving hospital, Maathai hosted the group in her home, risking arrest for holding meetings without a permit. Subsequent to several strategizing meetings, Maathai recommended a public march to the attorney general's office to deliver the mothers' demands. They were to bring their bedding as an indication that they planned on staying until the government acted.

On February 28, 1992, days after leading other women leaders in an impromptu march to Uhuru Park, where she placed a wreath to celebrate the death of the Times Media Trust Complex project, Maathai met with the mothers of political prisoners at the same park. She marched with them to Attorney General Amos Wako's office, where she also served as translator for the group, to present their letter of demands. At the meeting, Maathai told the attorney general, "We have come to give you this letter to request you as the official adviser to the government, to please advise our government that the time has come for all political prisoners to be released" (*Taking Root* 2008). The women, most over sixty years old, indicated that they would stage a hunger strike at Uhuru Park for the three days they gave the government to release their sons. In Wako's response, which began, "We may not necessarily agree that all the people you call political prisoners are political prisoners," he promised that the government would act. Awaiting his response, Maathai and the mothers set up camp for the hunger strike in a corner of Uhuru Park in downtown Nairobi. Supporters and sympathizers joined them, and allies donated tents and other supplies. With global media present and reporting, members of the public shared their personal experiences of mishandling and brutalization by government representatives and instruments. On Sunday, March 1, the same day Maathai named the vigil spot in Uhuru Park "Freedom Corner" (a name it maintains to this day), religious leaders held a big interdenominational service with the protestors at the park.

The government waited out the women's three-day ultimatum, expecting them to leave. They did not. On the afternoon of March 3, fearful about the enduring and expanding vigil and the political narratives being shared, government officials directed paramilitary police to disperse the protestors with ruthless force. In defiance, some of the mothers employed an indigenous practice of many Kenyan communities—disrobing as a form of protest. This was effective in halting some of the police action. Ruth Wangari Thungu, one of the mothers whose son was held at Kamiti Maximum Security Prison, remembers: "We were attacked brutally. Wangari, in particular. Luckily, I was able to help by quickly undressing. Naked, I fought the police and made them leave. . . . And that's how we saved the women" (*Taking Root* 2008). Maathai, beaten unconscious, was hospitalized once again. The vicious attack on the women instigated protests and riots across the city and condemnation from governments and human rights organizations internationally.

Undeterred by government orders to stay away, the mothers started returning the next morning, but finding the park and Freedom Corner under guard, they sought refuge at All Saints Cathedral, located next to the park. Church officials, led by Rev. Peter Njenga, the provost, allowed them the use of the basement, and they continued their stay-in and strike. When Maathai was discharged from hospital, she held a press conference, defiantly putting on record that she would not be silenced, and she rejoined the mothers, spending nights with them at the cathedral when she was not traveling or pressed to be somewhere else on personal or official business. As Thungu recollects, "We slept on the stone floor with Wangari Maathai" (*Taking Root* 2008).

On March 31, the mothers sought an audience with the president to deliver a petition but police blocked their advance. FORD members, including Maathai, called for a national strike to start on April 2. On the night of April 1, the mothers protesting with Maathai were awakened by hundreds of police, who invaded and occupied the cathedral grounds for days while the women barricaded themselves in the basement of the church. On April 12, the archbishop of the Anglican Church in Kenya, Manasses Kuria, expelled the police from the church grounds, allowing the protest to continue. Following this event, the women would often chain their bodies to each other, at Maathai's suggestion, a move intended to make them harder to separate and disperse in the event of an ambush. The symbolism of that chaining and physically attaching bodies to each other is powerful, and the imagery is open to many interpretations even from feminist perspectives.

During the eleven-month life of the protest, Maathai, GBM staff, and supporters printed and distributed educational and advocacy materials on the mothers' movement, women's empowerment and rights, freedom of expression, and democracy, while petitioning and coordinating material and logistical support for the protesters. Thousands, including prodemocracy leaders, attended the daily sessions of what was a continuation of the activities of Freedom Corner. Though the protest was grueling, it was eventually successful. The first four sons were released on June 24, 1992, and by January 19, 1993, all had been released. The mothers, certificate of endurance from Maathai in hand, finally left All Saints Cathedral.

At the time the last group was released from prison, Maathai famously referred to all of them as her sons (*Taking Root* 2008). Like her, many relatives and other supporters unrelated to the political prisoners viewed the prisoners as Kenya's sons and themselves as othermothers, fostering empowered and empowering motherhood as an action path accessible to most people. To recognize how mother-centered womanism is accessible to most women, one must consider the African conceptualizations of motherhood beyond biomotherhood. Achola Pala's delineated dimensions of African motherhood (2013, 9) indicate that mother-centered resistance is applied by many women in individual as well as collective action simply as part of day-to-day living and also as a philosophy of life. Among many African cultures, therefore, it is not a feminist stance; rather, it is a societal value. This once again draws our attention to Maathai's postulation that certain ethical standards and practices of African communities are avenues to decolonizing women's liberation movements, and they render some new formulations of feminism unnecessary. An example is the force of mother power that Maathai and allies drew from in foregrounding what has come to be called in recent years in Western feminism "matricentric feminism."

Maathai did not consider the restoration of the capacity of mothers as authoritative and autonomous providers for their families as new feminism but as reclamation of their position in indigenous communities as equal humans. In fact, she believed that honoring mothers' needs served society, as demonstrated by the fact that the RPP struggle was intertwined with other political and social struggles. It was also a nongendered movement in makeup (Maathai 2007a, 217–19, 226). It would be easy to characterize the RPP mothers' struggle as a women's struggle if one does not note that the activists, supporters, and issues were not gendered. Without such a lens, one might also miss the fact that the use of mothers' bodies as a protest tool is a value of societies, not women. It is in fact the accepted belief that to dishonor your mother dishonors your person and the society that makes this tool effective for protest. Further, the fact that the sons, as champions of democracy, were fighting not for rights limited to women but for the liberation of all Kenyans made the mothers' struggle every Kenyan's struggle.

Maathai's life and intellectual explorations used the mother identity not just to access information about the communities to be served but also as an identity central to the realization of equity in society. She posited that holistic efforts toward restoring impartiality required partnership and complementarity, including reintroducing men to family life (Maathai 2009b, 275–78). Indeed, she exposed not just the lost motherhood-related privileges but also the accompanying extra burden placed on mothers in the absence of fathers (Maathai 2007a, 13). In *The Challenge for Africa*, she portrays the beginnings of this as occurring at the same time as the colonial administration's machinations were "uprooting the African man and forcing him explicitly or by default to seek employment away from his home" (2009b, 275). Thus, calling for a reversal of this trend of absent fathers asserted the case for a partnership between the sexes in processes of rebalancing function and power in societies.

A study of Maathai's ideas and ideals regarding certain female bodies as a channel to their empowerment is an encounter with decolonial knowledge and activism. Her holistic brand of empowerment celebrates female bodies, identities, and knowledges without debating them in relation to or in opposition to male ones. Through this lens, we are able to imagine the symbiotic relationship between men and women, mothers and fathers in raising communities that are conscious of human rights.

Rights and Being Human: Resources, Knowledge, and Leadership

Focusing on personhood—the human and not the woman—Maathai located bodies of citizens and their production as resources. In an interview with Krista Tippett (Maathai 2006), she said, "The truth of the matter is we are all resources anyway. We are a human resource." Not recognizing women's personhood as equal to men's further degrades the former's worth, making them an inadequately tapped resource by society. In her words, "the biggest problem that we have had, especially in the women's movement, is trying to convince the other half that we are a very important resource and we do make great contributions, and therefore we should be respected, we should be appreciated, our work should be quantified" (2006). Note here the use of the phrase "the other half" to highlight the complementary conceptualization of the sexes discussed in the preceding section. In the same interview, she lamented the fact that women are taken for granted and "even very competent women are sacrificed at the altar of political convenience."

What Maathai captured as the biggest challenge in convincing "the other side" of women's potential as a resource is a situation exacerbated by many feminist initiatives' continued focus on womanhood and not personhood. Her ideals contend that processes of resituating the agency and autonomy of women also restitute recognition of equal utu. Through a decolonial lens, she referenced values of indigenous Kenyan societies where female members were facilitators of peace and security and controlled significant amounts of human labor, material resources, knowledge, and leadership. Maathai historicized the root causes of the loss of this power, which was also the process of the public reduction of women's utu. She referenced the matrilineal beginnings of the Gikuyu, explaining that women had gradually lost privileges, including landownership, through history (Maathai 2007a, 5).

Maathai underlined the effects of colonialism's introduction of title-deed landownership (Maathai 2009b, 227) and the institution of a cash-crop economy that occasioned redistribution of control over resources and restructured knowledge surrounding food wisdom as well as other wisdoms. Among other foundations, the cash-crop economy shifted opinions on the desirability of particular crops and degraded the centrality of subsistence farming to many agricultural cultures, which women initially controlled. Maathai captured the double effect of a heavily cash-crop-dependent economy on women. It at once disparaged the resources they controlled and started the process of devaluing their labor (Maathai 1995a). This abrogation of women's productivity and resource management corroded societies' regard for their equal utu socially, politically, and economically, redefining women as the weaker sex (Maathai 1994, 9).

The resulting assault on women's autonomy, along with the denial of equal access to formal education for women, furthered their relegation to the position of dependents in society, with limited influence even in the domestic sphere. Maathai noted that at independence, women found themselves attached primarily to domestic and welfare institutions previously maintained and run by European women, including the Girl Guides and the Young Christian Women's Association (YWCA). They were also directed to step into domesticating private and public institutions, estranging female members of society from leadership. This reduction of women's work and lives that had begun during colonialism continued after independence. Most notably, the devaluing of their labor and productivity contributed to debasing of knowledge and technologies controlled by female members of society. Making the case for repositioning women to their rightful spaces, the scholar observed life in the society of her birth as one where women controlled parts of farms, markets, and homes. Even through the colonial era, especially when men like her father were absent and working away from home for meager earnings from the colonizers, women sustained homes, families, and communities (Maathai 2007a, 13–14).

Through education and skill-development programs, the GBM sought to refabricate this control of resources and knowledge for women as a way to rebalance societies. Maathai considered women to be not just recipients of knowledge but a "tributary of knowledge" (2007a, 122). She demonstrated that among the Gikuyu, acquisition of knowledge that allowed one the agency to impact society began at birth. Right from birth, mothers and othermothers, as nurturers and protectors of knowledge, rooted a child in belonging and into responsibility for resources in their environment and community. The ceremony of the first meal that binds people to the land and its resources, described earlier, is especially noteworthy. It communicates that transmission of knowledge was not gender directed because children of all sexes underwent the same ritual (4). Maathai believed that the salvation of all human beings and their future world lay in honoring their inherent bond to the land and, based on that, their commitment to interacting with the environment in a way that sustained it and, consequently, them.

A loss of independent control over resources and knowledge left female members of communities particularly vulnerable and burdened. Maathai highlighted the impact of this loss on women in contemporary societies. She argued that most conflicts, which are simply struggles for the access to and control of resources or reactions to diminishing natural resources, heightened women's struggles (Maathai 2004c). She used the historical occurrences in Rwanda and the Democratic Republic of Congo as examples to illustrate that the most vulnerable and violated by the conflicts are women (Maathai 2009d). In another example, referencing a visit to Darfur, she said, "As long as we have all these conflicts, it is the women who will continue to suffer, so that is one reason why I guess as women we should really work for peace, because we know how painful wars can be to us and our daughters" (2009d).

In addition to reinstituting respect for women's utu through delivering control of knowledge and resources, a significant part of the GBM's and Maathai's work focused on addressing imbalances in the distribution of power by positioning female bodies in leadership. From the late 1980s until her death, Maathai was part of the political agitation to place more women in parliament and in public service, aimed at building a critical mass of women to influence policy and politics. Using Rwanda as an example, she elaborated on how a critical mass of women could be the key to changing the systems and creating a less destructive management of power (Maathai 2009d). Indeed, this was one response she offered to criticism about her failure to accomplish as much toward dismantling patriarchal structures as people had expected upon her entry into parliament and government. She acknowledged the reality of women entering a world created and run by men—that they have limited impact and sometimes have to play the men's game by rules created and maintained by men (Maathai 2007a, 254; Maathai 2006).

With others in the postindependence women's movement in Kenya, Maathai supported affirmative-action initiatives for and in parliament. With the GBM and along with other organizations in the women's movement in Kenya and across the continent, she supported initiatives to train and support potential women leaders for public office, from the grassroots to the national level. Her own vying for presidency was a statement on her views on women as leaders. In her Nobel Prize speech (2004c), she stated, "I am especially mindful of women and the girl child. I hope it will encourage them to raise their voices and take more space for leadership. I know the honor also gives a deep sense of pride to our men, both old and young." By including men in the celebration, this statement asserts that the advancement of women and rebalancing of societal power should be desirable for both female and male members of society.

Maathai's decolonial focus on African conceptualizations of inclusion and service to all of societies' members contests the idea of the Western feminist savior and disrupts the narratives and arguments of

Eurocentric feminism. Balancing privilege and degendering person-hood make possible the realization of human rights for all persons. This promotes the maximization of all society members' potential as resources for the society. Maathai's ideas and ideals insisted on the right to inclusion of women that was latent in the values of many indigenous African societies, arguing that a loss of that balance had negatively impacted development on many levels in African commu-nities. A return to some indigenous forms of organizing power and control would recoup some of that balance. With restored equity and balance, women can harness their capacities and their environments to ensure all people's sustainable liberation, autonomy, and empower-ment. For women, this would manifest as unbowed personhood in tune with their environment or what I term "decolonial eco-agency."

Decolonial Eco-agency and Unbowed Personhood

According to Maathai, actualizing agency and full personhood be-gins with getting off the wrong bus, based on what she defined as the wrong bus syndrome (Maathai 2009b, 3–8). To reclaim one's agency, she proposed, "You need to take action. . . . You want to plant, you want to empower yourself. . . . We say to go ahead and start to plant trees. Grow and produce enough food for your family" (Kennedy and Richardson 2004, 41). This defines eco-agential development. I define decolonial eco-agency as the capacity to harness one's environment as a pathway to cultural, economic, social, and political empowerment and societal equity. For this to occur, people must first understand their particular environments and their relationship to them as well as the relationships between their environments and other environ-ments. They must develop and constantly nurture that relationship and their environments. It is only in doing so that they can positively, effectively, and sustainably manage and use said relationships and en-vironments. Decolonial eco-agency, therefore, involves people taking care of the environment so the environment can continue to return the favor. Tapping into indigenous knowledge on environmental management can then offer solutions to challenges regarding suste-nance, health, education, and economic development, among others.

For Kenyan and African women, establishing decolonial eco-agency would start with the choice, discussed above, to decolonize their self-definition and liberation movements by applying the lens of utu. Key to this conceptualization of an unapologetically African personhood would be the shedding of Western definitions as well as measures of value. Maathai urged that African women in general "need to know that it's okay for them to be the way they are—to see the way they are as a strength, and to be liberated from fear and from silence" (Sears 1991, 56). The departure she encouraged was from Western typecasts of Africans promoted and sustained by the "internationalization of Western culture's patronizing and exploitative conceptions of Africans" (56). She proposed, instead, a return to particular indigenous African ways of doing to advance the reclamation of empowering locations of women of indigenous African communities like her own, the Gikuyu.

Maathai embodied the unapologetic being and doing of Africanness by African women not just in her rhetoric but also in her ways of self-identifying and self-fashioning. As she was a visual representative of African women with a massive platform, it was hard to miss her Africanness. Wearing her trademark African print outfits began as a way of representing it in a different way as a politician's wife to satisfy the patriarchal moralizing spaces influenced by "modernization" and religiosity (Maathai 2007a, 111). She would come to embrace this fashioning as an empowered expression of her Africanness. This way of relating to her aesthetic representation was in the same vein as her choice on her wedding day to wear "a beaded necklace with nine strings, which represented the married daughters of Gikuyu and Mumbi. It had been made especially for me, for that day" (109). The debate on self-identifying has been partially explored in chapter 1. On the subject, she resisted changing her last name to her husband's or using the tag "Mrs.," arguing that this was a practice introduced by the British and was not Gikuyu or African. She would capitulate to prove to his family that she loved him, first hyphenating her name and then dropping the hyphen (140). Upon her divorce, rather than drop his surname as he demanded, she opted to spell it to match phonetically with the Gikuyu pronunciation, adding an extra "a" to become Maathai (147).

Such a process of self-defining would reconnect African women to their environments because Maathai considered the bond between African people and the environment unbreakable (Maathai 2007a, 5, 44–46; *Taking Root* 2008). Thus, seeking what was positive about their roots, she argued, would by default reconnect African people to their complementary relationships and interactions with their natural environments. This in no way aligns with certain anthropological spaces' essentializing of the relationship between Africans and Africanness and nature. Rather what she presents is the symbiotic and respectful interaction between people and their natural environments. She contended that an absence of visibility does not erase the intrinsic reality that nature creates cultures, including human cultures, and that human cultures impact and recreate nature. Because of this, she considered the realization of human rights impossible without proper management of human and natural resources. Therefore, in this reconnection of persons to respectful engagements with their natural environments, and so utu, lay the women's salvation and that of their communities.

In Maathai's conceptualization, Africanist empowerment approaches, including those for women, are innately eco-friendly. Thus, philosophies of women's empowerment must intertwine ecological and womanist concerns. Rooted in African indigenous knowledges and cosmologies, Maathai fashioned environmental protection and sustainability as a tool for women's reempowerment (Maathai 2005c). Decolonial eco-agency makes use of the intrinsic and active bond between women and their natural and cultural environments and would allow for the contesting of current global circumstances, which leave women as the most negatively impacted by environmental degradation and also the least empowered by their societies. Indeed, following her attendance at the UN's First World Conference on Women in Mexico City in 1975, Maathai argued that destroying environmental resources was a direct attack on women's rights. Thus, a restoration of women's rights must be eco-directed. The GBM connected societal empowerment to environmental protection (Maathai 2009b, 2010, 2003, 2009d). The work of the movement in communities purposed to go beyond environmental management to ensuring access to basic needs, civic education, leadership training, and advocacy, among others (2003).

The GBM's success at the grassroots level and globally demonstrates the weight of decolonial eco-agency as a principle, which lies in its inclusiveness assured by its accessibility to most people. For example, Maathai noted that tree planting, a solution to women's challenges, did not require a degree, just bodies: "The tree-planting process [was] a wonderful symbol of hope. Tree-planting empowered these women because it was not a complicated thing. It was something that they could do and see the results of. They could, by their own actions, improve the quality of their lives" (2000, 30–39). Such immediate locating of potential to be a change maker in the hands of every woman is decolonial in nature and disrupts the dependency syndrome. Considered in tandem with Maathai's characterization of tree planting as civil disobedience, this positions women's bodies as complete and adequate to realize a level of resistance, liberation, and human rights protection. Augmented by female identities and bodies with protest power and authority to control some resources and knowledge, it antagonizes structures of the patriarchy. The GBM philosophy, whose definition Maathai envisioned and championed, and the movement itself exemplify the concepts of unbowed personhood and decolonial eco-agency.

I wrap up this discussion by returning to the decolonial and Afrocentric ideas introduced at the beginning of the chapter. Through this filter, it is important to appreciate that in many African cultures what made resistance and women's power sustainable was the fact that acts of resistance were embedded in everyday existence. Maathai's life work models a critical African approach to ensuring equity and human rights, which centers all people in society. By localizing the approach to center a specific cultural and political demographic, and in so doing producing it as a theory and practice that can be replicated across cultures, histories, and geographies, she offers the global potential of decolonial eco-agency. Such an approach is important to centering marginalized populations and feminisms within the larger academic spaces and global studies of women across disciplines.

4

Theorizing and Activating Utu Citizenships

Wangari Maathai framed leadership and citizenship as active and offered distinctive abstractions for contemplating old ideas and questions on democratic spaces and the challenge of good politics. Her
classifications of citizenships activated and performing at micronational, macronational, and international levels provide new frameworks and language for studying identities, democracies, nations,
and even borders. She is one of many scholars, including Godwin R.
Murunga and Shadrack W. Nasong'o (2007), Makau Mutua (2008),
and Norman Miller and Rodger Yeager (2018), who have historicized the character of Kenyan and African citizenships and leadership. The distinctiveness of her work, addressed in this chapter, is
that, along with contemplating other relevant components to this
discussion, she foregrounded the question of trauma and introduced
the constituent of utu.

The designation of utu applied in this chapter recognizes the concept as community and actively communal and collective. Micere Githae Mugo expounds on the idea: "I am because we are and because
you are, therefore I am," affirming utu as the "essence of being human
and demonstrating communal solidarity" (2011, xii). She goes on to
say, "The act of being human is in the affirmation of others' humanity. Without this we are a mockery of the human essence" (40). Utu,
understood as community and communal, dispenses individual and
collective responsibilities and relations within societies. Desmond
Tutu elaborates thus: "You cannot be human on your own. You are
human through relationships. You become human. . . . Ultimately,
we are human only through relationships. . . . We are really made
for this delicate network of interdependence. So that, the completely
self-sufficient person is in fact subhuman. I need you in order for
me to be me. I need you to be you to the fullest. We are made for
complementarity. . . . Ubuntu says, not you are human because you
think. You are human because you participate in relationships" (Tutu

n.d.). Maathai's view was that by focusing primarily on practicalities and operations of political systems and politicians, the question of psychological effects on the leaderships and citizenships of the postindependence African nations had not been adequately attended to. She weighed, for example, the trauma related to feelings of inadequacy, which new African leaders brought along as baggage, and the impact of that trauma on the creation of the cultures, identities, relationships, and psyches of the new nation-states. On this question, her work directs scholars and others to consider the extended trauma, paying attention not just to the levels but also to the feelings associated with deficient expertise and confidence that new leaders of independent African states possessed and how this shaped the formation of postindependence citizenships and leaderships.

The history of the problematic side of modernity—capitalism, imperialism, colonialism, and all their attendant ills—occasioned the maiming and violation of cultures, spiritualities, and persons across the African continent. People were dehumanized, relationships broken, heritages and ways of knowing decimated and vilified, societal structures and organization annihilated, and resources stolen. The emotional, mental, political, economic, physical, social, and environmental damage, wounds, and fallout from the colonial and postcolonial eras is what I define here as trauma felt at the individual as well as national level. I underline the political, economic, cultural, and psychological trauma and related effects experienced by both leaders and citizens, which Maathai posited as crucial to understanding postcolonial citizenships and leaderships in Kenya and the rest of Africa. I start this exploration with a look at her overview of African citizenships as products of colonialism and neocolonialism. Using her work—primarily the book *The Challenge for Africa*, speeches, and interviews—I track and define the crises of identities, citizenship, and leadership that materialized out of this history. Finally, I highlight the model she offered for evaluating and resolving these crises to delineate revolutionary leaderships, which would result from her prescribed revolution in citizenships. Through this journey, I draw attention to her steadfastness in applying conceptualizations of citizenship and leadership from indigenous societies of Africa toward advancing democratic spaces and sustainable development. I christen this citizenship, inspired by indigenous African cultures, *uraia wenye utu*, Kiswahili for "utu-centric citizenship."

Colonized Citizenships and the Erasure of Utu

In her speech at the UN's Fourth World Conference on Women in Beijing on August 30, 1995, Maathai stated, "Africans, like all other human beings, want to enjoy the basic freedom and rights. They want justice, equity, transparency, responsibility and accountability. They want respect and human dignity. They want a decent life and an opportunity to feed, shelter and clothe their families through honest, hard work." She characterized these as goals and desires intrinsic to African societies and not new postcolonial ideals. Indeed, she said, "Sometimes you may find that the human rights we are trying to advocate for now are human rights we lost through colonialism" (2009a). Per this perspective, the empowering of citizens of African countries must start with viewing democracy and sustainable development not as modern ideas but as fundamental properties of their societies. The following quote expounds this: "Another component in this revolution is for Africans to recognize that, while they may think they are 'better' than their ancestors by being educated and literate, and living in an age with motorized transportation, computers, and some modern amenities, if those ancestors were to rise from the dead," they would be shocked at the failures in justice, human rights, securities, and failures of leaders and citizens (Maathai 2009b, 155).

Grasping the idea of utu-sensitive democratic spaces as underlying indigenous modes of governance unlocks new schemes for analyzing and addressing the current binds experienced in crafting and performing leaderships and citizenships across the continent and beyond. Maathai's analysis, while highlighting the contributions of colonialism to the creation of prevailing political conditions across the continent, focalized a renaissance of indigenous political and democratic practices as an alternative and a solution. Hence, she purposed to explain how Africans had lost touch with these practices of civic life. Primarily, she indicted the colonial administration that wrecked and discredited indigenous self-governing processes and structures of African communities, a process accompanied by deterrence from observing indigenous religions and traditions, which were guarded by utu. Ironically, these utu-respecting customs and systems on which societal order was grounded were shunned as incompatible with Christian ideologies and teachings (Maathai 1995a). As indigenous modes of leadership were vilified and drained of power, no proper training in new ways of leading or

being citizens was offered. This created a dilemma for the postindependence leaders, the effects of which were to be suffered by citizens
who had for decades been forced to live as subjects of the Crown, at
best, second-class citizens.

In Maathai's estimation, it was inevitable, therefore, that there
would be challenges with instituting new citizenships and leaderships, as exemplified by outcomes of the elevation of young Africans
to leadership positions from which Africans were previously excluded
(Maathai 1995a). Indeed, as part of imperialist propaganda, they had
been advised that they were not good enough for these positions. In-
heritance of colonial governing instruments offered no preparation
for this new kind of leadership and citizenship. New leaders were
thrust into positions they were unprepared for and were required to
lead an undefined citizenry. Compounding the challenges faced by
new leaders was the fact that precolonial indigenous communities
had embraced communal governance within region-specific micronations. For them, the idea of the national had, until that point, only
been experienced as part of an oppressive colonial system, and so the
new leadership should have had the finesse and proficiency to define
a Kenyanness that all citizens could rally behind. This activation of a
new kind of leadership and citizenship needed due diligence and (re)
humanizing that did not occur.

Maathai accentuated a number of glaring shortcomings with these
new representatives and expressions of Kenyan and African leadership. First, they were students of colonial masters primed to take over
colonially defined national and regional spaces, administrations, and
institutions. Politically naive, they lacked awareness of the responsibilities and necessary tasks they had signed up for. Some, or their parents, had been gullible "corroborating students of the same colonial
administrators who wanted devotees of their philosophy and values to
govern the new independent African states. These were to be the cor-
roborators for neo-colonialism" (Maathai 1995a). Out of this history
was born a new breed of African elites—a small group that continued
to collude with the Global North to exploit the natural resources and
peoples of Africa (*Taking Root* 2008).

To sustain this corrupt jurisdiction of resources, absolute power
and control became necessary, animating a continued embrace of
colonial-era values and practices. Information production and flow
was controlled by the state, and punishment for any dissent was
rampant and brutal, not unlike practices of the imperialists. In Kenya,

for example, emboldened police reproduced abusive uses of the colonial kipande system. It was also necessary to keep the citizens divided in order to control them, which was an irony for a new state trying to nationalize. Ethnic identities were therefore constructed as oppositional to each other. As Maathai put it, "They have invented divisive and manipulative tactics reminiscent of the colonial tactics of divide and rule" (1995a). In this environment, disillusioned citizens, their trauma continually augmented, were forced to demand better governance (2009a). In response, many leaders employed totalitarianism and other dehumanizing practices. Journalist Njehu Gatabaki, who was arrested over twenty times, captures this loss of utu: "We were denied the basics, the fundamentals that make a human being what a human being ought to be" (*Taking Root* 2008). The outcomes of this state of affairs were crises of identity, citizenship, and leadership. Many internal conflicts and other ills of the totalitarian regimes have continued to create and aggravate these crises.

An application of Maathai's reading of these traumas and attendant crises reveals that a lack of grounding in any cultural or political philosophy that the entire nation could rally behind made the practical and psychological postindependence challenges hard to address. This disconnect from forms and values of indigenous citizenship and leadership denied both leaders and citizens access to empowered ways of navigating and managing the effects of colonialism and neocolonialism as well as encountering themselves. At the same time, there had been no investment in alternative approaches: the new citizens of independent nations had not been trained in what it meant to be a leader or citizen in a macronational form of democracy because they had never been participants in this form of democracy. Colonial governance was not a democracy, nor had they been considered full citizens within it. Additionally, following the independence of African nations, certain countries of the Global North, having exited traditional colonialism but wielding new interests, sacrificed attention to democracy in service to the Cold War as well as the need to maintain easy and cheap access to resources on the African continent (Maathai 1995a).

The crisis in leadership was evident in the birth of exploitative and oppressive government systems, sometimes even necessitating self-serving changes to constitutions. Single-party authoritarian regimes were born, some of which remain in place today, and dynastic presidencies are also common. President-for-life debates are still raging in some countries two decades into the new millennium. Maathai reasoned that perhaps certain African leaders hang on to power because, unlike in the West, there are no perks following the end of one's presidential term (Maathai 2009b, 117). In short, the new leadership on the continent was opportunistic and self-serving, and "the new black administrators and the bourgeoning elites enjoyed the same economic and social life-styles and privileges which the imperial administrators enjoyed" (1995a).

These failures in leadership informed the evolution of the citizens' sensibilities and identities, birthing citizenships in crisis. People of many African nations were directly and indirectly locked out of participating actively in democracy, and civil liberties were not just curtailed but brutalized with impunity. This, according to Maathai, "results in dangerous participation in citizenship" (1995a). Such a situation gives rise to either rebellious or passive citizenship, both of which are dangerous on a number of levels. Both passive and rebellious citizenship are reactive, not proactive. Both rebellious citizenship and passivity can threaten the security and survival of the nation-state in different ways (Maathai 1995a) and trigger mistrust on several levels. Take, for example, the failure to meet the basic needs of the people, which instigates and promotes corruption of individuals at all levels of society. This is especially so if the resources are selectively distributed to benefit small groups while others languish in poverty and neglect (Nierenberg and MacDonald 2010, 261–62). Materialism and social advantage drive unethical citizenships (Maathai 2009b, 41) as both groups—those in power and the marginalized—find reasons to engage in corruption and other ills.

Rebellious citizenship, manifesting in a variety of ways, occurs because, as Maathai noted, it is difficult to fight a dictator using democracy (Maathai 2009b, 115). On the other hand, continually let-down and traumatized citizens become jaded when their complacent or rebellious citizenships fail to deliver results. This breeds not just individualistic and self-serving citizens but also passive ones. To the mix of influences that helped construct traumatized and passive postindependence African citizens and citizenships, including colonialism, the Cold War, slavery, and cultural destruction, Maathai added religion (25–36). Foreign religions such as Christianity produced a cohort of citizens content to wait for God to resolve issues and for future judgment and rewards to be had in heaven; they even glorified suffering (40). Religiosity sometimes inspires passive citizenship, which also misconstrues good citizenship as acquiescent because "leaders are from God" and must be respected at all costs. In effect, the masses shirk their responsibilities as citizens in a way that they would be unlikely to within spaces where utu was the operating philosophy and where the sacred and the secular were inseparable, as in indigenous African societies. Religion can also become a simple escape—a coping mechanism for oppressed citizens.

The foregoing conceptualization of colonially constructed leaderships and citizenships informed Maathai's activist and scholarly ideas on this subject. In the next section, I look deeper into the three crisis areas I have identified out of excavations into her life's work.

Crisis of Identities

"The connection between who I am as an African and the abstractions of peace, democratic space, and development is deeper than words can say. In seeking restoration for my continent, I am quite literally restoring myself—as I believe, is every African—because who we are is bound up in the rivers and streams, the trees and the valleys. It is bound up in our languages, rich aphorisms from the natural world and our fragile and almost forgotten past" (Maathai 2009a, 287–88). This quote, which wraps up Maathai's *The Challenge for Africa*, captures that which was lost—and which, in part, characterizes an identity crisis.

Maathai defined the crisis of identity as happening on a number of planes impacted by imperialism, forces of globalization, destruction of environments and heritages, and erasure of indigenous ideals, spiritualties, symbols, systems, structures, languages, and knowledge. The definition of a citizenship in Kenya or any other newly independent country on the continent should have been a part of the exercises that sought to prescribe a national identity. The crisis of identities (Maathai 2009b, 184–92), discernible even recently in experiences connected to the 2007 and 2017 national elections in Kenya, she argued (192–210), in fact begins with a lack of appreciation for the nature and implications of the diverse identities that constitute the national. She explored the idea of the loss of cultural heritage as complicit in generating the superficiality of the modern African state (160–67).

Contending that erasing the tenets and ideals of indigenous communities weakens and eventually disintegrates communities,

Maathai floated the idea of micronations—very well-organized and well-structured societies—rather than "tribes," a term whose dehumanizing character she contested (Maathai 2006, 2009a). She referred back to the superficiality of the state inherited from colonialists, where the divide-and-rule policy deliberately and strategically emphasized the differences between the micronations. Embracing this postindependence reality without rewriting the narrative of community meant that the suspicion and bias between micronations endured. Indeed, the focus on one's own micronation to the detriment of the others is the continuation of colonial practice. Maathai stated that during colonial times, "we developed certain biases against each other, and we became very committed to our micro-nation, and we identify with our micro-nation. And when our micro-nation is threatened, we feel very threatened, much more than when the nation, the macro-nation, the nation that was created by the colonial power—when that is threatened. And I think every conflict you see in Africa is reduced to micro-nations fighting each other within that country because they do not fully identify with the macro-nation" (2009a). She proposed that people should be proud of their micronations and embrace them but at the same time appreciate that a micronation cannot survive in the twenty-first century independent of others because the politics and business of the world are organized and operate at macronational level. Thus, there is a need to work with the other micronations to ensure participation in matters of the world.

Maathai saw the erasure of cultural identities within a country as occasioning an adulteration of indigenous cultures, a position that simply repudiates cultural diversity, decimating heritages, including languages, political and legal systems, and religions. The conviction of many governments is that denying cultural identities breeds nationalism that is not biased or centered on ethnic communities. In fact, she argued, what it does is create a crisis of identity that cripples citizens. Not clear who they are, they are compromised in their capacity to participate in the national democratic spaces. Put another way, erasing people's identities does not engender informed or proud national-platform participation.

Micronations can be defined simply as primary-group identities of the people of many African countries. Within them, family belonging and clan organizations were underwritten, as were clear structures of leadership and governance, all safeguarded by institutions such as taboos and other traditional wisdom and spiritual and other cultural beliefs and existences that constituted utu philosophies in praxis. It is under these family, clan, and micronational systems that people are able to pinpoint their values, philosophies, rights and wrongs, preferences, and appropriate material and abstract cultures. An erasure of these value systems without replacing them with other tried and tested ones created the crises of identity and citizenship we explore here. This is demonstrated in scenarios where politicians easily co-opt the support and votes of large segments of populations based on an "us-versus-them" mentality. An understanding of citizenship values borrowed from principles of indigenous communities might give the masses the capacity to sift through the implications of the politicians' plans, recognize the reductionist way in which politicians are appropriating their identities, and resist.

With the breakdown of these utu-grounded micronational systems, it becomes especially hard to establish and initiate one's identity-related values nationally, especially under a system where the corrupt appear to be thriving the most. A lack of scruples and ideals is made attractive, even desirable. It is on these nearly forgotten individual and group values that Maathai rested her argument for the individuals' responsibility to their own community. She argued that "Africans have belittled or ignored the fundamental cultural and psychological importance of micro-national identity, instead using ethnicity for political gain" (2009b, 6). Therefore, she presented a positivizing of micronations (211–14) as having the capacity to mitigate some of the challenges of the crisis of identities and reverse the breakdown of communities (171–76). She noted, for example, that erasure of local languages was distancing people from the micronation, not bringing them closer to a national identity (221). She called for Africans "to rediscover and embrace their linguistic, cultural, and ethnic diversity, not only so their nation states can move forward politically and economically, but so that they may heal a psyche wounded by denial of who they really are" (6).

It is important to note here that on two occasions, in incidents unrelated to her statements on micronations, Maathai was criticized for promoting tribalism. The first, details of which I share later in this chapter, was in response to her involvement with communities in the Rift Valley following an outbreak of violence related to elections; the second was related to her activities within opposition politics and campaigns ahead of the 1997 national elections. As the 1997 elections drew closer, Kenyan women fought for change that served women through the Inter-Parties Parliament Group (IPPG), made up of representatives from KANU, the DP, FORD-Kenya, FORD-Asili, and Safina, an opposition political party cofounded by Paul Muite, Richard Leakey, and others in 1995. Just five weeks before the elections, on November 20, 1997, Maathai announced her intention to run for president. She came under fire and suspicion for that decision. This move to run for president was unpopular with some members of both the women's movement and the prodemocracy movement. She was accused of separatist politics and also of weakening the women's movement by running in an election where another woman, Charity Ngilu, was already one of the favorites (Maathai 2007a, 257). Some believed that Maathai compromised the campaign of Ngilu, who had been the only woman running until Maathai joined the race. Others opined that running for the presidency was at odds with her GBM work, which required her focus and service. That June, she had been named by *Earth Times* as one of the top one hundred change makers in the world in relation to the environment. Maathai maintained that she had only joined the race to put herself in a position to dialogue with fellow opposition leaders and push for fielding one opposition candidate. She made a further misstep when, in what she explained was an attempt to draw the opposition together so they could field a single candidate, she first approached leaders from her own Central Province. This, to some observers, appeared to be an effort to raise an opposition coalition from the province.

One can acknowledge the strengths of these controversies and still appreciate the astuteness of Maathai's theorizing on the place of micronations in defining citizenship and the contributions of its denial to the crisis of identities that is ever expanding in Kenya and other African nations. As mentioned above, the crisis of identity delivers the modern African state as a superficial creation (Maathai 2009b, 184–87). Citizens are "urged to shed the identity of their micro-nations and become citizens of the new modern state, even though no African really knows what the character of that modern state might be beyond a passport and an identity card" (46). In her valuation, the result is a compromised, limited definition of the macronational identity, culturally defined by dances performed at national festivities for politicians. She wrote, "Few African leaders recognize that what they call the 'nation' is a veneer laid over a cultureless state—without values, identity, or character. Those who would promote local cultures and practices are still accused of fostering 'tribalism' and division rather than unity" (46). Maathai proposed ways of reimagining community as an approach to managing the crisis of citizenship because failure to understand one's identities in the local or global milieu results in a crisis of embodying and performing contextualized citizenship.

Crisis of Citizenship and Reimagining the Idea of Community

According to Maathai, citizen identity and the concept of citizenship emerges from the argument that "without citizen participation and an active civil society, prospects for sustainable, equitable development are bleak" (2009b, 59). With the absence of governance cultures that foster citizens' participation in democratic spaces, agential citizenship is jeopardized. These circumstances raise questions related to what it means to be a citizen—a Kenyan, a Zambian, a Nigerian. Maathai's position was that to understand this or even begin to construct it in the service of good citizenship does not mean engaging with the question of what it means to be Luhya, Pokot, Luo, Gikuyu, Kenyan, or African; rather, it means seeking to be a community. She promoted reimagining "what it means to be a community—whether a micro-nation or the network of micro-nations that are countries, regions, and the continent itself" (215). Embracing the idea of community as a tool for better investigation and appreciation for micronational, macro-national, regional, and even global citizenship would serve citizens and leaders and also scholars who study these entities. By centering the idea of community, a number of things transpire. First, actions of citizens questioning and responding to both their responsibilities and that of the community at large and addressing their role as members of a community beyond themselves would have positive implications for sustainable development and democracy. Second, centering the idea of what it means to be a community fosters the reimagining of borders (215), which could be intercommunity within Kenya or on a regional level—for example, with the Economic Community of West African States (ECOWAS), the East African Community (EAC), the Common Market for Eastern and Southern Africa (COMESA), or the African Union (AU)—and even at the global level.

Citizens then raise or respond to questions on how they fit in as part of these local, national, and global communities; what their role is; and how their identities protect and serve, and are protected and served by, these many layers of community. How, for example, does their global citizenship exist alongside Kenyan citizenship and Luhya citizenship? Centering the concept of community would allow citizens to be allegiant members of micronations without erasing macronational networks, identities, and loyalties (Maathai 2009b, 217–18). Her simple contention was that, as human beings, we are always members of different communities at any given time, and they need not expunge each other. As an example, she offered a model within which such an approach could be grounded and employed to serve national interests, saying, "It would be a vital, boundary-breaking step if a nation established a forum for representatives of micronations that could be incorporated into the governance structure of the macro-nation. A sense of collective responsibility could thus be instilled among citizens throughout the country" (218–19). Some of these principles she applied in defining the GBM approaches and shared in the civic education workshops she conducted (Maathai 2003, 128–29).

Beyond the individual citizens, Maathai advanced the role of civil societies as collectives of citizens helping develop and sustain communities (Maathai 2009b, 156). This demographic would lead the citizens in holding the government accountable to the people's needs and correspondingly articulate government positions and developments to the people (156–57). In her book *The Bottom Is Heavy Too* (1994), Maathai described the need for civil society as a bridge between the people and those in power, because, for marginalized individuals at the bottom of the pyramid of political and economic power, upward progress is impeded by their circumstances. Through the GBM and other educational initiatives, Maathai was able to articulate the roles and responsibilities of citizens and citizen collectives at different levels of society.

Maathai's strong scholarly interventions defined an active radical utu-based and utu-informed citizenship, which is best illustrated by her own experiences with the Kenyan government and the resulting changes, shared in the following account with details drawn from her memoir, *Unbowed*, archival records, and media reports. In 1989, Maathai involved the local and global media, governments, and allies in her fight to save Uhuru Park, which then "covered only thirty-four acres" (2007a, 185). Plans were underway to build the Times Media Trust Complex, a sixty-story skyscraper intended to serve as KANU headquarters and the head office for the party's media mouthpiece, the *Kenya Times* newspaper. Other establishments to be housed in the tower included shopping malls, galleries, performance and meeting spaces, and offices. Along with this would be a massive statue of then-president Moi. All this was priced at about 200 million dollars at the time, financed by "a loan guaranteed from the government to private investors" (186). Maathai, with the support of the GBM, initiated a campaign to save Uhuru Park. Starting on October 3, 1989, in a campaign that included letters to the press, the managing director of the *Kenya Times*, global environmental protection organizations including UNEP, and relevant ministries and government offices in Kenya, she called for halting the project, highlighting the potential environmental, historical, social, and human impact. Realizing that the building would also necessitate the demolition of some historical buildings in the city, she sent protest letters to the directors of the National Museums of Kenya and the United Nations Educational, Scientific, and Cultural Organization (UNESCO) and the UNDP.

Maathai internationalized her campaign when on October 26 she wrote to the British high commissioner in Kenya, asking him to intervene by imploring the British partners and investors to pull out of the project. However, government officials, using the media, continued to market the complex as a viable and legacy-inspiring project. Maathai unrelentingly sent out letters to anyone she thought would help and vowed not to stop until some resolution was reached. This set off another battle of words between her and representatives of the government, accompanied by intimidation on the part of the government, requiring that her friends and partners were always vigilant to ensure nothing happened to her. Things escalated to the point that, on November 8, 1989, proceedings in parliament were halted to discuss Maathai and her international campaign, which representatives of the government argued compromised Kenya's position as a sovereign state. The attacks of members of parliament on Maathai went beyond the issues, turning personal. On November 15, contractors broke ground for the complex at a ceremony held at Uhuru Park. This progress and the attacks by leaders only fueled her fire. She continued writing letters, including one directly to the president on November 16.

Her campaign would progressively draw support from other individuals and organizations, including the Architectural Association of Kenya. Individuals also sent letters of support to her and to the media, protesting the project. Even with rising support, she suffered a high cost, including the disruption of her children's lives and loss of friends. Undeterred, at the end of November, Maathai sought an injunction from the High Court to stop the construction of the tower. With the courts' autonomy compromised because of influence from the executive arm of government, the case failed. She followed this up with a press release, again highlighting the concerns with the project and registering her protest. The tussle with the leaders continued even as the president publicly endorsed the project. Even members of the MYWO publicly condemned her, and there were demands for her to be expelled from the ruling party.

Maathai recalled that due to persistent harassment of her and the GBM, she was "becoming an outlaw in [my] own country" (2007a, 197). As part of that intimidation, in mid-December 1989, the GBM was ordered to vacate the government offices it occupied within twenty-four hours. The GBM did not have the financial resources to move to new offices, and landlords were not disposed to test the fury of the government by renting space to the organization. Not willing to let the GBM shut down, Maathai moved its operations into her house, a bungalow in Nairobi's South C neighborhood, from where the organization would operate for the next almost seven years. With a rising number of employees—up to eighty at one point—this left her and her son, Muta, only their bedrooms as private space.

Under these circumstances, she continued the campaign to save Uhuru Park, writing letters to influential people and organizations in various countries in the Americas and Europe. The press across the world, including leading newspapers, picked up the story. Eventually her efforts bore fruit, and the government of Kenya announced that the size of the project would be significantly reduced. Two years later, in February 1992, the project was officially dead. Maathai led a group of women in a celebratory march to Uhuru Park, where she placed a wreath to mark the burial of the project (Maathai 2007a, 203).

The foregoing, an exhibition of active and radical citizenship, was for many a watershed event in the history of Kenya. Dr. Ngorongo Makanga declared in *Taking Root* (2008), "It was a turning point, but most people could not imagine the courage of an individual who could stand up against this dictator. . . . That was the turning point in this country: that no matter how small, no matter what you are, you can make a difference." What Maathai perceived as important, therefore, was an investment in empowering citizens to activate their agency. Some ways she did this was through advocacy and training for environmental protection and replenishing and civic education, providing opportunities for ordinary people to ensure their self-sufficiency. Arming citizens with tools for the reclamation of autonomy and dignity was a necessary component as well as goal of positive active citizenship.

Maathai resisted the characterization of citizens as powerless subjects without know-how and at the mercy of patronage. She saw citizens from all walks of life, communities, classes, and religions as underengaged, possessing untapped reservoirs of innovation from which society could draw if only utu citizenship were activated. Radical utu citizenship is necessarily active citizenship, where individuals and collectives apply their citizenship in service to themselves, other human beings, and their environments. The goal of any community should therefore be to cultivate active citizens as agents of change toward democratic spaces and sustainable development, and who take responsibility for their own peaceful coexistence with others and their environment.

On the character of active citizenship, Maathai argued that "fundamentally, . . . Africa needs a revolution in leadership—not only from the politicians who govern, but from an active citizenry that places its country above the narrow needs of its own ethnic group or community" (2009b, 18). She explained the necessary purpose of citizens, through her own urging, to "challenge all of African society, especially its leadership, to break free of the corruption and selfishness that exists, from high offices to the grassroots" (5). This revolution, she imagined, was necessarily attended by a revolution of ethics (156). She said, "I do not believe that Africans are more intrinsically incapable of organizing their lives and asserting their rights, or more willing to accept bad leadership" (113). She outlined steps toward this revolution in leadership and ultimately toward an African revival (18–21), placing the responsibility for the revolution on an active, bold, fearless citizenry performing its duty through the vote and activism for democracy (Maathai 2005a). A refined understanding and appreciation of their identities as individuals and communities would ground good utu citizenship, which would demand good leadership. Maathai's conviction was that inspiring citizens to activate their citizenship would help in resolving the crisis of leadership and instituting strong democracies.

Crisis of Leadership

Wangari Maathai defined leadership as "an expression of a set of values; its presence, or lack of it, determines the direction of a society, and affects not only the actions but the motivations and visions of the individuals and communities that make up that society" (2009b, 25). I explored her ideas on the crisis in leadership and its roots and effects earlier in the chapter. To those points, she added that postcolonial African citizens experienced, as one of their major tragedies, their misspent trust in leaders who failed them over and over. What limits, delays, and sometimes totally prevents worthy development in African countries, she argued, "has its origins in a lack of principled, ethical leadership" (25). The crisis of leadership for African nations and their nationals has a number of components, which she outlined, starting with the ineffective, discreditable, coercive, and exploitative nature of the leadership inherited from colonialism (25–30, 44–46).

The first generation of postindependence leaders were "all born subjects of European powers" (Maathai 2009b, 45). Leadership, as they understood it, was defined by colonial masters, as imposed on the people and lorded over them. Active partnerships between the leaders and the people were not a valued pursuit. Immediately after independence, such leaders continued the abusive forms of managing the countries' people and resources that the colonialists had implemented, emboldened, and protected by the circumstances created by the Cold War (Maathai 2009a). Years after independence, Maathai observed that "while African leaders could have excused themselves for being unable to protect their people from the exploits of colonial empires in the 19th and 20th centuries, they can hardly escape blame for allowing neo-colonial exploitation, which continues to reduce many of their people into paupers in their own countries" (1995a).

As earlier indicated, to protect economic and political interests, foreign nations and partners maintained, and continue to maintain, relationships and support for bad African leaders (Maathai 2009b, 124). This has had a double effect, heightening the crisis of leadership and citizenship. First, the foreign powers create opportunities where they can control and benefit from African resources, an exploitation that continues to traumatize the people. Foreign governments that should hold corrupt African leaders to account, having abandoned their role, create new opportunities to control African spaces and economies. Second, some African leaders mortgage their countries to the hilt, even while they continue to facilitate large-scale corruption within. In these realities, the Global North benefits from delivering unfair loans attached to conditions and agreements that reinforce its control over African countries (49–50). On the other hand, African leaders, whom Maathai referred to in one interview as "leader-men," not leaders (2009a), realizing they can get away with their practices in the face of such latitude, make little effort to improve governance policies and practices.

The upshot of tolerating corrupt leaders who are blind to the needs of their people has been an ever-growing rift between the ruling elite and the masses, a situation that introduces another component of this crisis in leadership: that one cannot lead people one is disconnected from. It is this part of the crisis that is illustrated by the plundering of the national coffers without a care for the citizenry (Maathai 2009b, 25) or having the roads cleared of all cars so leaders can drive through unobstructed, while citizens sit in traffic for hours, and in some parts deal with broken-down, almost nonfunctioning infrastructure.

Crowning this crisis of leadership is the destruction of Africans' cultural and spiritual heritage, which allows for promoting the interests of some ethnic groups at the expense of others. Thus, spiritual heritages that would guide proper utu-based governance and leadership ideals are absent, and ethnic communities and identities are used only to separate the people for the benefit of those in power (Maathai 2009a). A crisis of and in leadership occasions circumstances that encourage inactive citizenship—pathology of power, the mentality of "our turn to eat," and pandering to ethnic and parliamentary constituencies—and this compromises development (Maathai 2009b, 114). It also produces ungrounded leadership, where leaders lack principles and seek only spaces that favor them, including changing political party affiliations at will or even creating new parties to ensure election. Another outcome is the focus on trappings, birthing a demographic called *wabenzi*—"people of the Mercedes-Benz" (123).

Maathai embraced an elaborate and expanded definition of democracy (Maathai 2009b, 56), where utu citizenship and revolutionary ethical leadership construct appropriately functioning communities and democratic spaces, which more effectively and sustainably make use of available human and natural resources to overcome challenges. In this space, leaders and citizens ensure protection and proper-value trading of the continent's resources. Governments expand investment in nurturing human and economic development (112–13), and citizens take care of their responsibilities to question, to agitate, and to elect leaders with integrity. In such an environment, "achieving a quality of life that is sustainable, and allowing the expression of the full range of creativity and humanity" becomes possible (56). Active communities that respect and celebrate humanity then emerge. She stated, "Such communities could ask themselves: 'Do we feel marginalized? Are we capable of acting in concert to make sure that our resources are used equitably? Do we recognize the value of belonging to a state? When we are entrusted to positions of leadership, are we committed to enhancing the welfare of our fellow citizens?'" (Maathai 2011a).

Maathai saw these questions as crucial to the realization of well-functioning communities. To serve the community, she advocated honest and proactive responses to the questions that would support the fashioning of "a system of governance that can evolve and change to meet the needs of the people over time" (Maathai 2011a). On how such communities could be defined and attained and what the measures of success would be, Maathai offered the three-legged-stool model for activating and testing democratic spaces and development. This model, which draws from the ethics and codes of indigenous African communities, can also serve as an instrument for analyzing democratic spaces and concepts in general.

Functionalizing Democratic Spaces: The Three-Legged-Stool Model

Maathai offered the imagery of the traditional three-legged African stool fashioned out of a single block of wood to symbolically model principles of good governance and revolutionary utu leadership and citizenship. Borrowing from knowledge of societal management and community building in indigenous African communities, she saw efforts toward generating utu-grounded progressive leadership and citizenship, as well as democratic spaces, as refashioning ideals that are inherently African rather than as new standards (Maathai 2009b, 55). She recalled a time before slavery, colonialism, Cold War politics, and neocolonialism when, in many African communities, the symbolic stool was fully intact (58–59) and lamented what had been lost with the erasure of respect for indigenous cultural heritages.

She elaborated on the components of the model. The seat of the stool "represents the milieu in which development can take place" (2009b, 57). The three legs signify (1) democratic spaces serving the rights of all people as well as the environment; (2) just, sustainable, and accountable administration and distribution of natural resources; and (3) cultures of peace. The legs of the stools are codependent and in constant dialogue with one another as cultures of peace create and promote human rights, social justice, respect for the environment, utu, reconciliation, compassion, and recompense. Within such a cosmos, citizens, assured of various securities within thriving democratic spaces that embrace equity as a principle, can enjoy education and perform productively and creatively. Such an active and empowered culturally grounded citizenry then invests in practices that lead to economic and technological revolutions. Thus, "the spirit of citizenry not only welcomes development, but drives it" (57).

Maathai applied a pragmatic lens to constructing structures that would safeguard a functioning three-legged stool. She observed, "The point to recognize is that, just as one develops technologies and expands the potential for breakthroughs in computer science and engineering through technical colleges, so advances in leadership and the application of values must receive similar impetus" (2009b, 155). She proposed as a feasible solution the application of indigenous African practices toward engineering these desired citizenships and leaderships. Initially, the revolution would require the installation of younger, more innovative leaders with a different mentality toward governance. Observing that many of the leaders of independent African countries have so far been products of a birth during colonialism and have embodied some values of colonialism, she raised the question of whether a new generation of leaders not defined by colonialism and colonial practices could change the narrative (125–28).

Maathai envisioned the installation of such leaders as part of establishing methods for developing new understandings and cultures of democracy and productivity. Such new approaches engender revolutionary citizen-leader philosophies and identities into which up-and-coming leaders are inaugurated and apprenticed. The outcome is citizen-leaders who appreciate their responsibilities as citizens, and so their position as leaders is not separated from the citizens they lead. She proffered *ituika*, a practice from the Gikuyu people, on which the apprenticing of leaders could be modeled (2009b,118–21). This inventiveness would resolve a number of issues, including ensuring the preparedness of new leaders. Along with apprenticing, Maathai advocated consultative leadership and the relinquishing of power after proper terms. Ituika involves group governance that cooperatively transitioned new leadership cohorts into power when the tenure of the old unit had passed. Ituika, which, she explained, directly translates to "the severance," were ceremonies that "served as de facto term limits." It guaranteed every generation an opportunity to contribute to the destiny of their people and ensured "checks and balances against corruption" (2009b, 120), making active utu citizenship and leadership inherent in the society's political cultures. The last ituika, which should have taken place from 1925 to 1928, remains incomplete after interruption by colonial forces.

Ituika demonstrated how these strategies could work in tandem to deliver new narratives for African civic life and political leadership. Maathai wrote, "In communities where governance and leadership resided in one age group, after a period of time in power the entire age group retired in favor of the next generation. This functioned seamlessly because, the elder generation were invested in apprenticing the next generation of leaders" (2009b, 120). Ituika countered the pathology of power as well as mitigated excessive and unearned deference to individuals (111–25). Indeed, the failure of a generation to perform good citizenship and leadership was equally the failure of the generation before it. Thus, political leaders at all levels, willing to model good leadership for the next generations of leaders and then relinquish power, ensured the sustainability of revolutionary ethical leaderships.

A fourth approach toward ensuring a functioning three-legged stool, service leadership, is exemplified in the first two (Maathai 2009b, 19–20). Maathai defined service leadership as people giving the best of themselves with honesty, hard work, commitment, and compassion (Maathai 2009d). Such service is the responsibility of both the leaders and citizens. These ideals and principles that she charted would facilitate the foundational strength of the three-legged stool representing the tenets of democratic and developmentally viable political entities and communities. This sustainable self-driven participation is demonstrated by events in her life, such as the one recounted below, showcasing service-driven leadership as well as radical utu citizenship.

The 1990s in Kenya were characterized by constant government clampdowns on civil freedoms in an environment and period of increased agitation for true democracy enshrined in the constitution. To manage the administration's anxiety, representatives of the government arrested and charged many with sedition and treason, which carried the death penalty. For Maathai, there could be no expectation that her run-ins with the regime's agents would cease in the new decade. She remained at the forefront of the struggles for a democratic Kenya, equality for women, and environmental protection. The 1990s began with an increased global profile for Maathai, who was recognized internationally as one of the leaders of these three movements. Through the decade, her identity as a politician to be reckoned with would materialize. While engaged in the fight for the release of political prisoners, Maathai maintained her active involvement in the prodemocracy movement and the activities of what was becoming a solid network of the Kenyan and African women's movements. The state, in turn, intensified its hostility toward her, curtailing the news coverage of her and her interviews in state-owned media. It is important to note that few alternative news sources existed at the time in the country. While some citizens celebrated her persistence, she received criticism from others, including some women leaders claiming she was pushing a personal agenda at the expense of fighting against challenges faced by women. The contention was that she was increasingly spread too thin with her commitments as Kenya moved toward another national election. The criticism was further fueled by the increase in her personal profile and responsibilities with global networks for environmental protection.

While Kenya technically transitioned to multiparty politics, President Moi orchestrated a change to the constitution to require that the winner of the presidency receive 25 percent of the vote in five out of eight provinces. This was meant to ensure his win because only KANU had the national presence to pull off such numbers. The government also stopped licensing new political parties and operationalized the Societies Act and the NGOs Act, which restricted activities of nongovernmental organizations. Ahead of the 1992 elections, ethnic violence broke out in Rift Valley Province between the Kalenjin, Moi's ethnic community, and the Gikuyu, who largely seemed to support the opposition.

The opposition had intended to field a single presidential candidate against Moi in the elections. Unable to agree on one candidate, its members went down a path that would set the prodemocracy movement back years. In August 1992, barely a year after its formation, FORD split into FORD-Asili and FORD-Kenya, under the leadership of Kenneth Matiba and Oginga Odinga, respectively. Former vice president Mwai Kibaki, who had been minister for health, had resigned from government to form, with John Keen, the Democratic Party of Kenya on December 25, 1991. The opposition was thus splintered three ways. To reconcile the fragmenting opposition, some members of FORD formed the MGG, with Maathai as chair and the GBM as its operating base. Their goal was to achieve compromise and agreement on one candidate to mount a robust opposition against Moi's reelection. Maathai, along with other MGG members, held teach-ins for the public on democracy, governance, multiparty politics, and the role of the opposition all over the city, including at All Saints Cathedral and in a tent in downtown Nairobi. Additionally, with Dr. Ngorongo Makanga, Rev. Timothy Njoya, Paul Muite, and others, she founded the Movement for Free and Fair Elections. This organization, in partnership with the GBM, the National Council of Churches of Kenya (NCCK), and the Catholic Secretariat Justice and Peace Commission, translated election and party promotion materials into indigenous languages, offered civic education workshops, and hosted prodemocracy meetings and open forums.

In the end, the failure of the opposition to unite, along with KANU's machinations, handed Moi, in Kenya's first multiparty elections in twenty-six years, another term as president with only 36 percent of the vote. Six women were elected to parliament and prepared to start their term in January 1993.[1] Just days after the mothers of political prisoners ended their strike, and one day after parliament welcomed its first opposition members in twenty-six years, on January 27, 1993, Moi suspended parliament for almost two months at its first meeting, claiming that the house needed time to agree on an agenda. In fact, KANU needed time to court the loyalty and the support of some opposition members.[2]

With parliament suspended following the 1992 national elections and election-related violence not addressed, communities still settling preelection and election-period differences reawakened ethnic conflicts in parts of, then, Nyanza, Rift Valley, and Western provinces. In response, the GBM hosted workshops in some areas, highlighting the interconnectedness of resources, human rights, and security. Maathai and the GBM dedicated time and resources to spreading information on the violence, particularly that perpetrated against the Gikuyu people in the Rift Valley, where she had spent her early girlhood. She implicated the government in fanning the violence against the Gikuyu and protested the lack of action toward quashing the conflicts. Her choice to primarily consider violence against the Gikuyu came under condemnation for its ethnic focus and not just from members of the government.

Starting in February, Maathai made reconnaissance trips to the Rift Valley, where her team interviewed citizens and printed and handed out leaflets with information about her findings. In a February 1993 speech, President Moi reprimanded Maathai for distributing leaflets, accusing her of inciting ethnic violence against the Kalenjin. KANU members of parliament joined Moi in denouncing Maathai. Maathai's riposte was a letter to the president, copied to the press, detailing her work and reiterating her plea that the government act against the violence. Her team continued its work, which involved facilitating dialogue, hosting community team sports, and communal planting of what she christened "trees of peace." She established a volunteer service for resettlement and education of people displaced by ethnic clashes, and her team leased land for some displaced people so they could engage in farming, their primary economic and subsistence activity before the conflicts. The regime employed the weight of government to impede Maathai's access to areas and persons affected by the violence. She reported that she would sometimes sneak into events organized by others, including government officials, to listen or speak. At one such event in Burnt Forest, the program was halted once her presence was discovered.

The events of the foregoing account, the story of a struggle toward restoring the three-legged stool, demonstrate Maathai's ideas and ideals on principles of revolutionary leadership and active citizenship outlined in this chapter. She posited that a successful revolution restoring the three legs of the stool would support the realization of a macronational identity while celebrating micronational identities. In her estimation, the stigma on celebrating micronational identities would be erased since it would not be accompanied by marginalization of some community members or inequitable distribution of resources and opportunities. Citizens as leaders and leaders as citizens would place national interests ahead of ethnic interests, with the ultimate result being peace and security for citizens, who then would feel free to continue activating more engaged citizenships. Citizens, she said, "must grasp the available opportunities and not wait for someone else to magically make development happen for them" (2009b, 19). These types of active citizens petition for accountable, transparent, and ethical governance. They demand policies and principles that celebrate cultural heritages and work to establish their relevance in today's world (20). She declared, "I don't believe that the peoples of Africa are more accepting of corruption than those in other nations. Africans can—as history shows many have—rise up and demand an end to inappropriate behavior. However, they want to know that if they stand up or speak out, then many others will do the same—especially their leaders, who should be in the forefront of this revolution in ethics. This is one of the most crucial challenges Africa faces. Meeting it could secure a value far beyond the dollar amount of any current or future development assistance" (2011a).

To her way of thinking, a truly free citizenry would be active, and a truly active citizenry would be free to fully engage with all aspects of their cultural, social, spiritual, political, and economic selves. When citizens and leaders, as stakeholders, assume ownership of the revolution, they create environments for robust opposition to international interests plundering Africa's resources. They support the establishment of fair markets and trade relations, with dynamic and entrepreneurial African actors (Maathai 2011b, 19). This can expunge the constructed dependency of African countries on foreign entities and serve as a path to freedom to self-identify, which contributes to the project of eradicating neocolonialism. As Maathai said, "So these three pillars, the pillar of peace, the pillar of the environment, and the pillar of democratic space, are extremely important for any state that intends to be stable. For when a state rests on these three pillars then the basin of the seat becomes the space, the environment, the milieu in which we can do development. Here we can meet as donors, as states, as financiers. We feel secure, we feel safe, because we are resting safely on those three pillars" (2005).

Revolutionary utu leaderships and citizenships, necessarily accompanied by a revolution in ethics for all players, would support the reconstruction of the three-legged stool. Scholars and policymakers can conceive of other applications of the three-legged-stool model in activating and studying democratic spaces, justice, and development in the nation-states of contemporary Africa and the world.

Wangari Maathai delivered new language and frameworks for engaging the topics of this chapter. Her work, which, as the Nobel Committee noted, "contributed to drawing attention to political oppression—nationally and internationally" (Norwegian Nobel Committee 2004), can inform the study of African and global political communities. Maathai conceptualized democracy as a space where freedom was realized in all dimensions. I have used the phrase "democratic space," a preference of Maathai's, instead of "democracy," aligning with her observation that "democratic space gives us a space to be ourselves, a space to be creative, a space to be self-respecting, a space to feel good about ourselves, a space to dream, and a space to aspire. We can do all that if the three pillars are safe" (2005b). She saw this kind of liberation, maintained by investments in cultures of peace and utu, as a sure path to delivering fair and just governance. The challenge is how to institute value systems that recreate the functionality of the three-legged stool sustained by engaged leaders and citizens (Maathai 2009b, 60–61). To this, her work offered an answer: "Government ministers, university professors, civil society activists, development specialists need to be involved in crafting policies and legislation both within and across our countries' borders for utilizing natural resources sustainably and sharing them more equitably" (14–15).

5

Just Globalization

Utu and Development as Social Justice

Wangari Maathai addressed the unceasing reinvention of "underdeveloped worlds" and the attendant oppressions and marginalization. She identified as "perhaps the most unrecognized problem in Africa" (2009b, 129) a disempowerment that breeds erasure of self-confidence, trepidation, feelings of jadedness and apathy, and ultimately dependency, which benefits the Global North (76–77). This is a significant part of the fashioning of the underdeveloped world. Africanist scholars of political science and international relations have made observations and arguments similar to some of Maathai's explored in this chapter. However, I focalize her unique positions on rebalancing globalization through a model of development that centers utu and social justice to erase what I call politics, language, and philosophies of "underdeveloped Africa."

I outline her framing of prevailing international relations and structures of globalization as continuing to recreate the idea and reality of "underdeveloped Africa." Maathai envisaged this underdeveloped Africa as existing alongside Africa. The latter is a continent rich in natural resources where, as she noted in her 1995 speech at the UN's Fourth World Conference on Women, citizens of African countries, like others, desire a decent life with the opportunity to take care of their needs and those of their communities through honest, hard work. They want participatory and credible democracies that respect civil society and governance that is committed to all forms of security for citizens. They do not aspire to underdeveloped world citizenship or characterization and profiling. Maathai wanted Africans to be reminded of the newness of underdeveloped Africa, urging them to recognize that the "majority of their forebears were honest, fair, and just, and that their societies were functional and people's basic needs were met—and challenge themselves to emulate some of these values" (2009, 154). She observed, "Part of the tragedy of Africa is that ordinary Africans don't, for the most part, remember and take pride in this history" (154).

With this lens on Africans and what would be christened "Africa" as a space that predated its Eurocentric constructions, Maathai interrogated the politics of meaning-making that inform the production of hierarchies of bodies and worlds—first or third; developed, developing, or underdeveloped; civilized or uncivilized. For African countries and their people, the "underdeveloped" filter offered by the voices of the "first world" drowns out their self-representation, definition, and voices and presents the continent as incapacitated (Maathai 2009, 77–82). These meaning-making processes regulate power dynamics within institutions and thought systems to continually produce the conditions of the underdeveloped world. It is these negotiations of space, power, identities, and different types of capital, as articulated in Maathai's work, that I outline in this chapter, charting the invention of underdeveloped Africa as a breakdown in utu, humanness, and the pathways she proffered for reversing this and realizing a more balanced, humane, and just world. Micere Githae Mugo aids our understanding of this argument with her elaboration on utu: "I do believe in truth—meaning, at the most basic, the historical, materialist reality that confronts us whether we want to acknowledge it or not. This reality either affirms our humanity, or denies it. Because of this, I also feel that it is a human responsibility to make clear proclamations when negation diminishes the human being in any of us. . . . I believe that refusal to make a proclamation in the face of injustice and oppression of other human beings is evasion of a human responsibility" (2011, 43). Mugo further maintains, on living with utu in a globalized world, "I subscribe to it—heavily! I tell you, don't listen to anyone who suggests to you that this kind of thinking belongs to 'primitive' and/or 'communist' societies. Every human being should have this as a life motto" (230).

Inhumane Globalization and the Invention of Underdeveloped Africa

Population increase across Africa has often been identified as a chief culprit causing many of the continent's challenges, including unemployment, food insecurity, and lack of development. Maathai posited other, more significant, causative factors, offering particulars such as although "industrial" countries had, at the time, only 20 percent of the world's population, they consumed 25 percent of the world's resources. This she saw as having more potential for inducing the deprivation of those in the developing world. A less-populated Africa, she argued, would maintain its marginalized position as long as the world embraced a globalization imbued with disparities and injustices (Maathai 1995a), which are safeguarded by national and international policies (Maathai 2009b, 3). A success story would therefore only emerge from African nations reempowering themselves to contest multifaceted foreign and domestic intrusions deliberately introduced to erase their political, economic, and cultural autonomy and power (Maathai 1995a).

The extant imbalances of globalization both produce and sustain insecurities and oppressions of certain groups of people, countries, and world regions in ethically questionable and unjust ways. In this section, I explore a number of these, starting with the systemic and systematic extermination of Africa's human resources. As noted in previous chapters, histories of slavery and colonialism disastrously impacted communities in Africa. The interruptions caused by colonialism and slavery resulted in failures in development and imperiled the nurturing of community members' productivity (Maathai 2009b, 275–77). In Kenya, as in other places in Africa, the breakdown of extended families, fragmentation of societies, and erasures of indigenous technologies and knowledge modified production cultures as well as production capacities. Maathai examined what she called "the necessary evil for the provision of labor" (276) and the colonial administrations' lack of sensitivity to African families, especially African men's need to provide emotionally and physically for their families. This inhumane disposition also left women in many African countries bearing the extra burden of raising and providing for families alone. Societal roles, responsibilities, and structures disintegrated, and while white men were praised as virtuous and responsible for taking care of their families, African men were sent away from home in service to the the Crown as civil servants, teachers, and clergy and to work on settlers' farms. Supplementing the inhumanity of estrangement of families, labor systems were punitive, and men's labor was exported from their communities to serve other people at minimal gain instead of serving their own communities (276).

Restructured modes of thinking, production, and distribution formulated communities that were easier to take advantage of during colonialism and after independence. During colonialism, to avoid competition, colonial administrations calculatingly prevented Africans from getting advanced formal education and from joining the professional classes. This ensured a lack of active participation by Africans in the definition of knowledge and societal systems and structures during colonialism and contributed to failed leadership at independence, as explored in chapter 4. In the newly independent nations, where Africans had been denied opportunities for training, there were "few local people qualified to manage the inherited colonial bureaucracies, or medical and service professionals to operate health services, the business sector, schools and other institutions" (Maathai 2009b, 30). This, in part, secured African countries' dependency on countries of the Global North.

The deliberate societal reorganization involving the degeneration of communities and communal modes of living affected the people psychologically and influenced ideas about resource management, distribution, and associated practices. The indigenous conventions of reciprocal responsibility between the individual and the community gave way to individualism, which supports what Maathai referenced as the winner-takes-all mentality (Maathai 2009b, 20–21, 30). The popular "our turn to eat" ideology that emerged from this reality has created a climate where individuals and communities seek to maximize the draining of public resources when a member of their family or community is in power, at the expense of other citizens and communities (Maathai 1995a). This kind of leadership and citizenship promotes an abuse of capitals and corrupts human resource coffers.

African leaders' failure to recognize and invest in their countries' human resource coffers carries forward colonial-era miscarriages of justice. In colonial societies, the creation of "less astute" humans and groups of people grounded othering relationships between the people and authorities. It also justified and sustained locations of "different bodies," which was reflected in the absence of equity in the control and exchange of goods, technologies, and ideas, a situation that remains today. Maathai located the human being as Africa's strongest resource (Maathai 2009b, 274). She observed that unless those at the table of decision-making worked with the people at the grassroots across Africa—the masses whose labor and day-to-day practices impact the economy and development—not only was sustainable development impossible, but also regression was inevitable.

Maathai opened her book *The Challenge for Africa* with a focus on the individual represented by the farmer of Yaoundé as the basic unit of Cameroon's human resource coffers. She used the farmer's struggles with soil erosion and predictable desertification to accentuate the effects of African governments' failing to invest in, empower, and partner with citizens (Maathai 2009b, 13–14).[1] In this she captured, as she did elsewhere, the financial, educational, security, and resources-support responsibilities of the postindependence African governments to their citizens. Maathai stressed the importance of strengthening the three pillars discussed in chapter 4 to ensure stable states "where people are appreciated, governments are investing in people rather than in weapons, they are investing in education, quality education, giving people the skills and the technology they need in order to exploit the resources that are within their borders, that's a state that feels stable, that doesn't feel threatened. Then it is able and willing to invest in its people" (2005b). Global partners, she argued, shared responsibility for this oversight related to investing in human resource coffers. As she noted, hardly any of what is received in aid and donor funds goes toward empowerment, protection, and the development of human resources. Instead, priority is tendered to development programs, which are lucrative for international communities, while forcing African nations into unmanageable debt (Maathai 1995a).

The resulting circumstances exacerbate discontent, which leads to further taxing of human resources through brain drain. Maathai called attention to the irony of Africans leaving a rich continent to live in near poverty elsewhere, working at menial jobs beneath their training and expertise. This, in her judgment, was inhumane and wreaked havoc on the psyche of Africans. Addressing the needs and freedoms of those who choose to leave the continent, she presented brain drain as a human rights issue (Maathai 2009b, 278). She correspondingly questioned the commitment to human rights when donor countries and the World Bank give "aid" to African countries and then lure away the trained individuals expected to run and develop the very institutions they finance. Maathai advocated fighting against "a continuation of the dynamic whereby the industrialized world provides Africa with assistance on the one hand and removes its natural capital on the other" (279).

This enfeebling of human resources has been accompanied by an ongoing crippling of systems on the continent, which is both deliberate and inadvertent—another way imbalanced globalization is activated. Maathai appreciated the enormity of the challenge to tackle this five-century historical burden, which has damaged Africans economically and politically but especially culturally and spiritually (Maathai 1995a). She saw the challenges before Africa as having moral, spiritual, cultural, and psychological components (Maathai 2009b, 3–4) stemming from centuries of maltreatment and exploitation. Eurocentric ways of thinking, many developed for the purpose of othering and disempowering so colonial powers could take advantage of African peoples and resources, positioned Africans and their communities, and eventually their nations' political, social, and economic systems, as inadequate. This has contributed to the continuous reproduction of the underdeveloped Africa narrative in practice and rhetoric and the image of the abject African waiting to be saved by first world entities.

African leaders play to this script, bowing too easily to coercion to rely on capital from the Global North and copy its development model under the instruction of experts and "mentors" from Global North bodies and countries (Maathai 1995a). In Maathai's consideration, the constant urging of African nations to imitate the financial systems and practices that enriched the West have impoverished African countries because no real thought went behind such encouragement or the attempts by African nations to live up to these recommendations (Maathai 2009b, 7). She argued that it was futile for Africans to attempt to reproduce the development paradigm of the West, contending it was illogical to believe "that Africa can also develop and catch up with the West even though Africa has no masses and colonies to exploit and no people to enslave" (1995a). This abuse of utu is the inhumane history in which unjust globalization is rooted.

While facilitating the compromising of human resources and systems of what are referred to as developing worlds, some of those so-called developed world entities appropriate the natural resources of African nations. This is another way unjust and imbalanced globalization is reproduced and sustained. In a 2006 interview, Maathai problematized the question of right to resources, highlighting the inhumane nature of resource grabbing that leads not only to impoverishment but also war. She observed, "People who live in such [highly industrialized and rich countries] have a feeling that even if they don't have resources within their borders, they can get them from wherever those resources are. But even if you can buy those resources, even there, there is a limit to what extent you can get those resources and not create a conflict." In other words, there is nothing humane about tapping to exhaustion a people's resources while being well aware that this could lead to conflicts and loss of life.

It is the fear of a strong civil society that would demand accountability from its leadership and for proper resource management that keeps leaders, local and global, in cahoots to not empower citizens and resource coffers of African countries. Instead, they continually introduce and promote ideologies and practices that keep citizens separated. Local leaders, for example, provoke ethnic nationalism that endorses blind following from citizens, supporting the leaders to retain privilege and power politically and economically (Maathai 2009a, 1995a). Indeed, as Maathai explained, "the tribal agenda today has to do less with problems of identity and ethnic nationalism and more with the issue of political survival, economic control and diminishing national resources" (1995a). Some Global North countries, on the other hand, in league with some African leaders, sponsor conflicts financially with weaponry, military training, and even peacekeeping aid. Such aid is almost always related to their interest in the exploitation of resources.

Further heightening this lack of consideration for utu, human rights, and lives is the role of some developed nations in funding the very wars that the draining of resources in African nations by outsiders has helped cause. Present here is a layering of multiple injustices as African countries, in this scenario, then help finance the arms industry of these Global North nations (Maathai 2009b, 109). With those arms, these foreign powers control the so-called underdeveloped Africa it has helped create, keeping it just unstable enough to allow for continued ravaging of the resources. Today, borders are open physically, technologically, culturally, and intellectually, and so globalization means that natural resources, as well as human and technological resources, are increasingly controlled globally by just a handful of people. Because of the imbalances in access to financial and other resources at the end of colonialism, few Africans had the capacity to competitively enter industry and production as owners. Africans as individuals and as states then had to try to break into industries already controlled by outsiders. Therefore, how, how much, when, and where Africans participated in production and trade was and remains highly regulated largely by foreigners.

The very people who had unjustly colonized Africans outlined how independent African nations and peoples participated in trade and economic systems domestically and internationally. The conditions of Africa's trade relations to the larger world have been informed by a number of things, including instituting policies that prohibit African nations from participating in industrial production, which forces African nations to remain natural resource producers. The Global North and other economic and political powers utilize raw materials and ideas from African countries to enhance their own manufacturing industries and then sell mass-produced consumer goods back to Africans at high prices. This importation of mass-produced goods has compromised the participation of African people in wealth-generating economic and knowledge-production enterprises (Maathai 2009b, 95). This imbalanced relationship is sustained by yet another unjust reality—inequitable open-markets agreements (101).

African nations have been encouraged by international financial institutions to produce raw materials and cash crops for international consumption. Maathai argued that this focus on raw-material production continued a practice of colonialism. Developed nations encouraged this limiting definition of the role of African countries at the same time as they promoted open markets and free trade. In this relationship, African nations open their markets and then spend what little money they have buying goods produced from raw materials acquired cheaply or at no cost from them in the first place. There is no reciprocal equitable opening up of markets of these economically and politically powerful foreign countries to African businesses and other economic interests (Maathai 2005c). Maathai stressed the need to eradicate these economic injustices, stating, "We have a special responsibility to protect our people from exploitation, to protect the resources that are in Africa, God given, and to make sure we do not allow ourselves to continue being the continent that provides raw materials to the rest of the world at a price we do not set, then buys the goods produced from the developed world at a price we can barely afford. That is economic injustice, and we would want it to be put on the table, to be fair and just" (2011b, 2).

Maathai demonstrated the inhumane nature of unfair trade relations and how these affect other securities, including food, internal, and national security, using the narrative of the fishermen of Angola. During a visit to Luanda in 1982, she observed that local fishermen were no longer fishing in their waters but large trawlers from the Soviet Union were. These commercial organizations that had decimated the Angolan fishing industry through supporting their war would take the fish to their country and ship it back frozen for sale to Angolans (Maathai 2009b, 83–85). Maathai's concerns highlighted the lack of utu attached to this and similar practices in three ways. First, she condemned as unjust the practice of foreign countries aiding in the creation of different crises, which they then later send "aid" to resolve in ways that earn them ideological, political, and financial profit. It is abusive, for example, for "donors" and "donor nations" or their citizens to have had a hand in creating, through their business practices, the very poverty they seek to now aid in resolving. Second, she questioned the "good faith" of humanitarian efforts that wait for people to suffer before offering support, when that support was always present and could be invested in avoiding the need before it occurs (86–89). It is not humane to wait for people to starve or die before offering help. Third, she pointed out the inhumanity of returning substandard goods as humanitarian aid to people whose high-standard raw materials foreign countries and industries had siphoned.

This interrogation can be applied to other areas of aid presentation, as she demonstrated in the following areas. In relation to health aid, she questioned the failure to avert preventable endemic diseases such as malaria through offering support for development to citizens instead of waiting to deliver international intervention after epidemics. Furthermore, she raised questions about the improper use and administration of that aid when it finally arrived (Maathai 2009b, 63–77). She also illustrated the injustices of some interventions in her fight against the introduction of genetically modified organisms (GMOs) to African countries' agricultures. Whether or not one agrees with her ideas on GMOs does not diminish the value of her arguments. Her position was that GMOs created perfect environments for killing resources because, first, the seeds are not native to the soil and so might devastate the environment and could be "harmful to biodivergence, to the farmer's own seeds" (2005c, 38). Second, because international bodies controlled the seeds, the production of local nations and farmers would be held at ransom as they are forced to get their seeds from Monsanto.[2] The bioengineering and patenting of seeds disadvantaged farmers in developing nations, especially since, as she noted, these companies could be insensitive (38). The failure of this approach in combating poverty and hunger, she theorized, lay in the fact that people across the world were not necessarily hungry because there was no food but rather because they could not afford the food that was available. Accordingly, making inaccessible the most basic stage of producing food—the availability of seeds—was unjust, inhumane, and dehumanizing.

Maathai highlighted the injustices in these trade arrangements, tendering that forces of the liberalized free market and capital flow sanction and normalize the sidelining of efforts from within African countries. This is because these agreements create conditions that favor outside investors. The investors and multinational companies also have massive political, social, and economic capital reserves, with which the locals are incapable of competing. Her following statement on unfair trade practices and processes directs us to consider development as social justice: "Without an enabling national political leadership and an international public opinion which considers it immoral to support that type of business, Africa is likely to remain exploited and marginalized by such inequitable and unsympathetic world trade" (1995a). Regarding this as a question of utu, justice, and human rights opens up new ways to debate issues of aid and humanitarian initiatives.

Having successfully created an "impoverished" Africa by degrading its human resources, natural resources, production, and trade, the Global North and other economic powers instituted another inhumane practice—commercialization of African poverty. When developing nations are coerced to play in unfair markets and then borrow from the very creators of those markets, their progress toward successful extermination of poverty becomes even harder to realize. African countries dominate the list of poorest countries in the world (Maathai 2009b, 267, 274). Maathai defined poverty as a lack of securities and resources, manifesting at the national and personal levels (63–71; Maathai 2003, 126–27). She, in agreement with promoters of the sustainable development goals (SDGs) (Sustainable Development Knowledge Platform), granted that the "rest of the Millennium Development Goals [MDGs] will be much more difficult to realize in Africa, unless you can address MDG number 1, which is ending poverty" (2011b 2).

Maathai contended that "African governments should be responsible and accountable to their people, lifting them from ignorance, diseases and poverty, which cripple them" (2005d). However, with resources, systems, and heritages of knowledge incapacitated, and unfair trade devastating African countries financially and politically, the prevailing environment falls short in attempts to resolve issues such as HIV/ AIDS, poverty, corruption, illiteracy, unemployment, environmental degradation, and conflict resolution (Maathai 2009b, 10), all enumerated as areas of urgent concern in the MDGs and SDGs. With systems turned dysfunctional, the "mentoring" Global North and other economically powerful "partners" help themselves to the resources of developing countries while offering unfair aid packages, perpetuating the inhumane regeneration of poverty and underdevelopment.

The securities and sovereignty of developing nations are further compromised through inhumane and unjust debt. Most aid disbursement is self-serving, and the circumstances of unfair trade discussed above, burdening debt, and policies and unfair agreements with development "partners" (Maathai 2009b, 101) result in profits flowing out of the supposedly underdeveloped countries. As Maathai explained (2009a), it should accurately be described as trade and not aid if every dollar invested in Africa as "aid" returns as four dollars. She referred to such aid as disguised trade. Furthermore, international institutions such as the World Bank and the International Monetary Fund often influence dictates that create "the political and economic environment in which they prefer to do business" (1995a). Maathai submitted that aid that is used as a form of ideological, financial, or political control is not only inhumane but immoral and unethical, a failure in utu. The creation of such dependency is its own form of colonialism. While Maathai was in support of censures against corrupt and undemocratic African governments, she condemned global governance that was contributing to the debt burden of African nations. In an interview in *The Progressive* (2005c), Maathai noted that, at the time, Kenya spent about 40 percent of its income servicing debt to foreign bodies and countries.

Noting the relationship between power, debt, poverty, and aid (Maathai 2009b, 90–94), Maathai questioned how humane the practice of foreign aid as it stands today can be adjudged, and she underlined the cruel nature of some forms of humanitarian support. Her point was that if in fact aid is humanitarian support, it would be more benevolent to cancel the debt, especially in view of how much has been appropriated from the developing world by these same countries delivering the aid. With such cancellation, these countries being "aided" could use that money to service development that could make future borrowing unnecessary. An avid critic of global governance systems, Maathai served as cochair of the Jubilee 2000 Africa Campaign. Jubilee

2000 was a global movement agitating for forgiveness of poor countries' debt by the year 2000 (Collins 1999). Emphasizing the callous character of the debts, Maathai argued that they did not benefit the poor people who continued to bear the brunt of suffering occasioned upon the country by those very debts. She elaborated, "When such countries are denied debt relief, it is the many poor people who are punished" (2005d), while those who are guilty of corruption do not suffer.

Compounding the insensitivities discussed in the foregoing is what Maathai explained as the failure of African leaders to advocate for their people domestically and on the global scene (Maathai 2009b, 23, 285–87). She blamed the calamitous economic hardships that Kenyans and other Africans faced on poor governance by both the local governments and global bodies. During the Cold War, the active redirection of allegiances toward foreign powers exposed African nations to ideological, economic, and political control from both sides. Even more damaging, it compromised the capacity of African leaders and nations to focus on building continental and regional connections that would strengthen their bargaining power against foreign nations and bodies. Economically and ideologically functional alliances of African nations could have negotiated better and more balanced opening-up of markets through the World Trade Organization (WTO). The power of the EAC, ECOWAS, COMESA, and other regional bodies has not been fully activated and leveraged for better global placing of African nations economically and politically because of national allegiances to various Global North partners (104–6). With a strong active partnership, African nations could contain the pilfering of African resources by outsiders as well as address matters of urgency for African people, not as defined by the Global North and other partners but by themselves. Such issues of urgency, according to Maathai, include a lack of basic needs, refugee crises, migrations, environmental degradation, sustained hunger and malnutrition, political instability, internal ethnic conflicts, diseases, and low life expectancy (Maathai 1995a). Many of these remain unresolved because African nations have been robbed of their say in formulating and implementing their development policies and agendas and because African leaders are not invested in changing the status quo. Maathai noted that "throughout the continent there are instances where forward motion and stasis are occurring simultaneously: efforts to battle corruption have been waged but often incompletely; principled and visionary leaders are still too few in number" (2009b, 11). In a C-Span interview (2009a), she described African leadership as mainly made up of a very specific elite, educated abroad, who unfortunately return with not just knowledge but also Western values and an appetite for a lifestyle "that cannot be sustained without exploiting the people and . . . without allowing a lot of the resources of Africa to be exploited at the expense of the African people." In her view, what is necessary is leaders who can take advantage of the help of the foreign partners without selling out their people or heritages.

Foreign countries and organizations, often in alliance with a few African ruling elites, influence the outlining of policies that affect the social, economic, and political lives of people of African countries. These elites, benefiting as individuals, continue to sell, as development, destructive policies, including heightened military spending, legacy political projects, and approaches that encourage the mismanagement of resources and corruption. Maathai faulted ruling African elites who collude with foreigners in business and politics to create "underdeveloped Africa," where one of the richest continents in terms of resources has some of the world's poorest populations (Maathai 1995a; 2009b, 267, 274; 2005d). Still, she argued, "greater private investment and capital flows, however, are not panaceas for underdevelopment" (2009b, 103). Efforts toward utu-driven humane and just globalization would be the way to effectively eradicate these challenges. This is because inhumane systems and policies that force people to constantly be worried about basic needs stand in the way of real development.

Maathai saw the oppressive circumstances and relationships that continue to burden African peoples and nations as happening from both inside and outside. While citizens of many African countries lament marginalization experienced from within the nation-states, the leaders compound their own people's oppressions and also produce circumstances that make marginalization and oppression of African nations by outsiders easier. Ergo, the creation of the "underdeveloped Africa" narrative has many authors, both African and non-African. Thus, the constituents responsible for sustaining the African underdevelopment discussed in this section must collaborate in ensuring its erasure. In Maathai's words, "It is not an easy battle to fight because five hundred years is a long time to struggle against all forms of oppression" (1995a). However, she stressed the necessity for investing in this fight, observing, "The repayment of debts, the realignment of trade, and the capitalization of African economies all depend on a rebalancing of globalization" (2009b, 104).

In the following section, I explore development as social justice, the approach Maathai proffered toward rebalancing globalization. This approach to development is easy to imagine through the lens of utu.

Rebalancing Globalization and Development as Social Justice

Maathai's interest was in defining ways in which African nations could deal with the issues explored in the first section of this chapter, realize balance and equitability in their positioning in relation to other countries, and hold on to their own heritage while maintaining touch with globalization as an inescapable reality (Maathai 2009b, 101–4). Acknowledging what Africans and others in the developing world want, she conceptualized new ways of looking at development, arguing that justice and sustainable development are not merely related but are in fact part of the same idea and that both are inseparable from the performance of humanness, utu. In *The Challenge for Africa* and her Nobel Prize and 1995 Beijing conference speeches, she outlined this relationship and conceptualization of development and globalization. She stated (1995a), "As we speak about commodities and communities it is important to be concerned about justice. What is the truth about Africa's international debts? When does stealing become a crime at the international level? . . . So much burden is being placed on the Africans by the international community and the African leaders appear incapable of protecting their own people from such exploitation and indebtedness." A morally, economically, and politically just world would embrace what Maathai called "pro-poor development." In such a world, citizens of developing countries would enjoy human dignity, respect for basic freedoms and rights, justice, equity, transparency, responsibility, and accountability (1995a). In other words, there would be an absence of "underdeveloped world" narratives and realities, and the presence of an embrace of utu. Through this filter of development as social justice, I outline here Maathai's thoughts on realizing globalization that is just, humane, and balanced.

Maathai conceptualized humane development, expressed and experienced at personal, national, regional, and international levels, as a means to rebalance globalization. She cited the interconnectedness of world issues and the fact that "Africa has been maligned and ridiculed by the same people who have exploited it and under-developed it" (1995a). Based on this, she offered insight into the kinds of cooperation and equal partnerships required at home and from international communities to counter the historical effects that shaped underdeveloped Africa as an idea and a reality. Equating societies to machines, she wrote, "Because modern societies are so complex and multilayered, most of us have little idea how the societal machine operates beyond the parts that most affect us. . . . If individuals are more inclined to do things that bring the machine to a halt or a crawl, eventually everybody becomes a victim. This is called underdevelopment" (2009b, 130–31). In this environment, "even the smallest move forward appears to take forever, and the societal machine is under constant threat of stopping altogether" (131). Effective intervention requires a vision that sees the larger picture: how the parts and constituents of this social machine interrelate and impact each other.

The Global North and other world powers, while continuing to create underdeveloped Africa, condemn the economic, intellectual, political, and social cultures within their invention. At the same time, African leaders and governments are complicit in the production of these cultures. Maathai suggested therefore that the onus was on the international community to put out more balanced, nuanced, and positive representations of Africa and also on Africans not to offer narratives of dysfunction (2009b, 80). In her interview with Marianne Schnall (2009d), Maathai stated, "I want to blame the world, but I also want to say that African leadership has also failed because quite often they have been found wanting in practicing good governance, responsible governance, free of corruption and misuse of the resources that are available." She similarly outlined responsibilities for individuals and civil society (2009b, 156). Maathai made it clear that her goal was not just to criticize the international community for the ills outlined above but also to push African nations and people to overcome passivity, fatalism, and failure by eliminating the dependency syndrome (5).

With everyone playing their part under systems grounded by the philosophies of utu and just globalization, African nations could expand development, reduce the dependency syndrome, and have a voice in the rebalancing of globalization to expunge "underdeveloped Africa" narratives, identities, and politics. Maathai promoted a pragmatic people- and community-centered, pro-poor model of development toward just and humane globalization. The bottom-up, pro-poor model of development as social justice that she proposed would amplify voices of Africans, focus on African solutions to African problems (Maathai 2009b, 144), restore Africans' control of African resources, diversify production, restore respect for African heritages, and enhance education. I delve into her elaborations on each of these in the paragraphs that follow.

Rebalancing globalization requires amplification of the voices of Africans. This would offer opportunities for decentering the usual spaces where voices *on* Africa are registered, including project progress and evaluation reports, websites, books, development plans, newsletters, and magazines. Many of these, which focalize "underdeveloped Africa" imagery, are generated by expatriates, representatives of international communities, and donor and aid agencies to serve their own purposes (Maathai 1995a). These sources, Maathai argued, needed "to present a vision of the Africa they wish to see rather than using images that undercut the very mission they are trying to accomplish. It should be possible for potential donors to respond to images of a functioning Africa that deserves support and not only given in response to those images that inspire pity and condescension" (2009b, 81). African countries deserve support because it is humane and just, given the centuries-old history that produced underdeveloped Africa, impoverished to a large extent to feed processes of globalization directed by powers outside Africa. This is a position Africans can articulate better than anyone else. As Maathai expressed it, a commitment by African governments to changing the rules of the game was necessary and urgent to the rebalancing of the game, which has for a long time been one-sided (279).

Maathai called for a revolution where African nations and peoples contest international interests and coercions that would acquire Africa's natural resources without paying fairly for them (Maathai 2009b, 19). Development of a revolutionary leadership, stronger civil societies, and the creation of partnerships and networks between African nations—for example, making travel and trade between countries on the continent easier (282)—would institute a stronger, more directed continental voice. Some of these developments are finally being pursued actively in the current millennium. Such a partnership and voice would influence or spearhead global and continental efforts to promote peace; political, social, and economic justice; sustainable management; and equitable distribution of resources, human rights protection; and democratic governance (Maathai 1995a).

Calling for this type of restoration of agency for African nations, Maathai declared, "We must make our choice or others, less sympathetic, will make that choice for us" (Maathai 1995a). Solutions to challenges for African countries continue to be fashioned by the outside world. Maathai proposed a centering of Africans and African solutions on issues affecting Africa as a way to erase the dependency syndrome. She suggested that Africans should not blindly take directions from outsiders but instead do their own thinking and acting toward resolving challenges facing their countries and continent (Maathai 2009b, 7). She said that if hegemonic Global North and other powerful external forces constructed Africa as part of the underdeveloped world to benefit their interests, it was asinine to expect them to be the ones to deliver redemption and empowerment (Maathai 2009a). Maathai advocated an understanding of empowerment that centers the marginalized and not their savior-perpetrators. In her view, empowerment that is motivated and primed by Eurocentric outlooks that demean African people cannot work for Africans. The injustice and dehumanizing nature of this kind of "empowerment" is clear in the fact that it is a reproduction of the "white man's burden" of colonialism. I locate Maathai's definition of humanitarianism and justice as utu. Humanitarianism as the performance of utu redirects focus on to the valuing of humans and human life and activates what Maathai saw as that which defines our humanity (Maathai 2010, 16) in service to the welfare and dignity of other humans. Justice as utu demands fair treatment for all people and consideration for distributive, procedural, and other fairness rooted in what is right and humane. It goes beyond rights enshrined in the laws of the land to critically, equitably, and humanely protect different forms of rights and punish wrongs.

Maathai highlighted the irony of the contemporary white "savior" (Maathai 2010, 113–17), emphasizing the fact that if balance is restored within globalization, then some leading economic and political world powers would have to acknowledge needing African nations and people more than the Africans need them. The foreign savior, essentially trying to return that which it has stolen from Africans at a premium interest and with conditional ties, is in fact a double or triple bandit. Maathai said, "Such stolen wealth should be retrieved and returned to the creditors. This could be a great economic humanitarian intervention for Africa! And it could be one way of alleviating poverty and underdevelopment in that part of the world" (1995a). The return of that stolen wealth is necessary to restore human rights and social justice. She said that any serious efforts by the international donor community to help African nations must involve compelling banks in donors' countries to account for what essentially is money in their vaults gained from stolen African resources. At the same time, the countries from which the money was stolen must demand its return (Maathai 2009b, 94).

Maathai presented as even more socially unjust and ethically problematic the practice of these saviors waiting to deliver aid instead of putting in place efforts to ensure that such aid is never necessary in the first place. Preventive measures are more humane and just, as well as more efficient, than humanitarian missions after the fact. Preventive approaches are more effective and cheaper, and they ensure the protection of human and natural resources, which, if lost to disease, war, or hunger, further erode development efforts and the human rights of individuals. Preventive approaches are, in fact, a key element of rebalancing globalization. However, because such a fair approach would curb the dependency cultured in the developing world and the control enjoyed by the Global North and other economic and political powers as a result of that dependency, the developed nations with interests in Africa and other developing countries invest instead in fashioning instruments to maintain the status quo of imbalance. They establish policies that sustain the impoverishment of African countries and finance civil wars. As Maathai noted, "Hardly any of the friends of Africa are willing to tackle the political and economic decisions being made in their own countries, and which are partly responsible for the same horrible images brought to their living rooms by television" (1995a).

Giving control of Africa's resources to Africans would help ensure that these resources benefit the people of Africa and curtail the dependency syndrome. Safeguarding the rights of African people to the resources of their lands positions African countries as free rather than coerced partners. In this environment, clear responsibilities and accountabilities can be laid out for businesses wishing to operate in African countries or with African partners (Maathai 2009b, 268–73). For Maathai, just and humane development demands accountability, which "must mean local, regional and international institutions working in concert to ensure that the industrialized countries do not repeat the sins of the colonial period, and extract without genuine recompense or an eye to protecting the resources of the future" (268).

Once control of resources is restored to the rightful people, Maathai noted, it is important to diversify production. Relying primarily on natural resources, Kenya, like many African nations, developed very few other industries for years after independence. Failure to diversify economies meant that countries could not renegotiate relationships or create new relationships with trade partners. Because of this, they are often bound in imbalanced associations with their existing trade partners and donors, limiting their autonomy and influence on policy, trade, and aid agreements. They then become simply suppliers of raw materials for others. Diversifying production would "present Africans with opportunities to increase their standard of living, expand intra- and inter-African trade, and develop their economies beyond the extraction of natural resources and the export of commodities. Indeed, Africa has an opportunity to add value to those commodities by generating finished products" (Maathai 2009b, 102). A lack of investment in training and augmenting of human resource coffers exacerbates the situation. Maathai explained: "The problem is that many Africans lack knowledge, skills and tools to create wealth from their resources. They are unable to add value to their raw materials so that they can take processed goods into the local and international markets and negotiate better prices and better trade rules. Without that capacity, opportunities will continue to slip by or others will continue to take advantage of them without the benefits reaching the people in whose name these negotiations take place" (2005d).

A lack of diversity in economies erodes bargaining power. It also impacts development in a number of other ways. First, it reduces the need to build industries. Industrial growth is a marker of economic and infrastructural development. Second, countries give up opportunities to expand employment prospects for their citizens through growth in industrial production. Third, because the jobs that line up with their skills and training are not accessible with few industries present, expertise in certain areas ships out of the country as part of the brain drain. Finally, economic growth is curtailed as the countries give up occasions to produce and market finished consumer goods.

Maathai explained that if African countries continued to rely on agriculture and failed to diversify their economies into production industries, they would quickly exhaust the sustainability of their agricultural production. They would deplete the productivity of the land, especially with continuing population increases (Maathai 2009b, 237–38).[3] With the land exhausted, there would be no way to provide many of the raw materials that are now the backbone of these economies. The enduring exhaustion of African lands for the benefit of foreigners unjustly creates conditions that promote and ensure continued dependence on these outsiders. Development of industrial production in African countries remains impeded so these countries can continue to be suppliers of raw materials and buyers of industrially produced goods from the outside. Maathai encouraged sustainable environmental use accompanied by a focus on existence beyond subsistence (11–18). She saw this not as an Africa-only issue but as an urgent problem for the globe, arguing that the continent maintaining its position of being simply a provider of resources for others in Europe, the Americas, or Asia would be detrimental for both Africa and the rest of the world (20). With the depletion of resources, not only is production for industry compromised but the danger of more conflicts also increases. The richer "partners" sponsor the wars, and the cycle continues. Therefore, Maathai advocated that African people resist pressure from outsiders and focus on managing and using their lands sustainably.

The assignation of tags such as "first world," "developed world," "developing world," and "underdeveloped world" is mostly based on advances, which today manifest in democracies, productions, technology, and innovation. Another approach Maathai encouraged toward rebalancing globalization is the creation of environments within African nations that supported creative innovations to ensure they remained technologically at par with other countries. She saw this as especially important because technology increasingly directs commerce, politics, and culture (Maathai 2009b, 19). However, she stressed that it is necessary to expand production and innovation in these areas through a balance of pursuing innovation and finding relevance for African heritages in today's world.

Maathai called for a renaissance of African heritages and valuing of African people's past and new knowledge. Processes of deculturalization that continued after independence (Maathai 2009b, 44, 160–67), and the resultant erasure of indigenous technologies and education, in many ways also affected Africans' ways of thinking about themselves as people lacking the capacity for innovation and technology. This was actively dehumanizing to African people. Maathai advocated looking back to move forward (154) and appreciating indigenous technologies, which would restore to the people and the world the identity of Africans as innovatively astute people. She emphasized that Africans and others have failed to recognize the significance of understanding and applying African cultural heritages in fully appreciating African identities and Africans' sense of who they are.

Because systems and practices of government and governance, agricultural production, cultural and natural heritage, and ecology are all "dimensions and functions of culture" (Maathai 2009b, 161), Maathai saw any innovation and development as a function of culture. She outlined the limits of cultureless attempts at development thus: "The tenets of modernity—with its belief that material goods, greater technology, and innovation at any cost will solve all our problems and meet all our needs—are insufficient to provide an ethical direction for our lives" (162). In other words, it results in utu-deficient, unjust globalization. To rebalance globalization, it is imperative to recognize the value of othered knowledges and philosophies, which would allow developing nations equitable opportunities to acquire and develop new ideas and technologies.

For the kind of industrial and technological innovation and creativity discussed above to be realized, a war on illiteracy is necessary. An influential part of Maathai's life was her work toward educational empowerment. She advocated for government investment in education and specifically more emphasis on technical and technological education (Maathai 2005d).[4] She outlined in several of her publications and speeches her views on appropriate approaches to education and the eradication of illiteracy. I elaborate here on her ideas on education, technology, and innovation as pathways to sustainable development, highlighting her skepticism about the economically powerful countries' commitment to sharing technologies with African nations. As with the raw materials, she argued that these countries preferred keeping Africans as simple consumers of technology and not developers (Maathai 1995a). For just partnerships in the area of technological transfer and development to be realized, she held that it was necessary to renegotiate relationships.

Maathai supported bidirectional knowledge and technology transfers between the developed and developing worlds.[5] Placing responsibility at the feet of both the nation-states of Africa and the international partners, she advocated for fair and broad sharing of technology, technological assistance, and technological education with African countries at affordable rates. She also encouraged African governments to invest in science and technology initiatives and to support cultures and environments that promote innovation (Maathai 2009b, 102).

Elsewhere she suggested that without investment in skills and education, "people will always find themselves locked out of productive, rewarding economic activities that would give them a better share of their national wealth. They find themselves unemployed or underemployed and they are certainly underpaid. . . . They get trapped in a vicious cycle of poverty and sometimes crime" (2005d).

Tackling this state of affairs would result in citizens of African countries thriving and regionally and globally activating their under-tapped potential and creative energies. These creativities can then respond to challenges and tasks related to the achievement of faster development on the continent. To this end, Maathai submitted investments in peace, environmental sustainability, and democratic spaces as approaches to the creation of stable states. In such states, governments invest in people and not weapons. They allocate resources toward good and appropriate education and technology so the people are equipped to adeptly harness the resources in their environments (Maathai 2005d).

Maathai argued that it is in the interest of the global community to erase "underdeveloped Africa" and elevate countries on the continent beyond being providers of resources for development in other countries (Maathai 2009b, 20). To achieve this, nations of Africa and international communities need to focus on development that empowers citizens of African and other countries to responsibly, equitably, and sustainably benefit from their precious ecosystems and rich natural and cultural heritages, while at the same time preserving them. African nations and partners would have to promote entrepreneurship of citizens of African countries, create global conditions and policies that mitigate unfair competition, and build economies based on servicing areas that are of interest to people across the globe (19). Additionally, any decisions reached with or by international bodies should involve strong African voices and be delivered to a leadership that is committed to development as social justice. This requires investment in developing strong human resource banks through education and training and also creating environments that discourage brain drain and encourage balanced technology transfer (278), development of innovative technologies, and industrial production.

Maathai captured the spirit of just globalization grounded in utu, calling for a compassionate, unifying, and tolerant global ethic "with values which give meaning to life experiences, and, more than religious institutions and dogmas, sustain the non-material dimension of humanity" (1995a). Such an ethic, instituted through globally influential bodies such as the UN, she said, needed to filter into all aspects of social, cultural, political and economic life (1995a). She suggested that committing to such an ethic would combat global power games, as well as materialism and individualism, and their associated ills, including "anarchy, egoism, hatred, injustices, violence and intolerance" (1995a). In her estimation, a holistic humanistic approach applied from the conception to the implementation of development initiatives was essential for just globalization (Maathai 2009b, 20).

Because of the multifarious nature of the challenges of an unjust globalization and because of the history that brought the world to this point, any rebalancing must admit some truths and affirm the valuable resource that is African people, heritages, and natural resources. While the international bodies problematize issues related to rebalancing globalization, African nations and leaders must come to some realizations and actions as well for the journey to be completed. Maathai (1995a) presented that it "is important that a critical mass of Africans do not accept the verdict that the world tries to push down their throat so as to give up and succumb". To all stakeholders, her lesson is worthwhile: "If we manage responsibly, with accountability for our decisions, if we promote human rights and justice, we are more likely to pre-empt many of the reasons why we fight." A just and humane development model and balanced globalization would seek to promote sustainability, empower people, save lives before they are lost, and recognize a shared human dignity among all people. A just development caters to this shared human dignity and would obliterate notions of "underdeveloped Africa."

6

Scholar-Activist Legacy

To conclude this book, I will examine the extent to which the ideas, ideals, and scholarly and activist legacy of Wangari Maathai have been preserved, actuated, or regenerated and suggest opportunities for extension of her work. The awards and honors she received from different institutions across the globe and the list of boards and global bodies she served, which I have logged in appendix 1, present an inventory of the causes and subjects to which Maathai devoted her life. They allow us to track the institutional channeling of her work and ideas and its implications in terms of the agendas, policies, and advances she impacted. The question of whether or not her work and ideas were of value to the world is moot in light of these recognitions. What demands attention, an objective this book seeks to contribute to, is the creation of opportunities for continued engagement with Maathai's critical thoughts within and beyond the academy.

It was not my intention in conceiving this book to take a position for or against Maathai's ideas and ideals. Rather, my goal was to distill and outline her thoughts and philosophies for easier expansion, application, critiquing, or testing. What emerged from efforts to consolidate her ideas on specific areas was a suite of weighty concepts, philosophies, models, and theories worthy of further examination and functionalization by scholars and activists. Societies across the globe continue to grapple with challenges related to women's rights, human rights, democracy, environmental justice and protection, and globalization. The critical thoughts charted in this book have the capacity to serve in the designing of solutions, knowledge production, activism, policymaking, and leadership in these spheres.

I will examine in this final chapter the location of Maathai's ideas and ideals as institutionalized legacy—that which institutions sanction and facilitate. Utilizing the agenda outlined by the Assembly of the African Union (AU) in "Decision Recognizing the Life and Work of Wangari Muta Maathai," I will inventory and assess efforts to preserve her scholarly and activist legacy. The AU's decision was passed at the Assembly of the Union's Eighteenth Ordinary Session, held in Addis Ababa in January 2012. With the decision, the AU sought to create a framework for memorializing and institutionalizing Maathai's philosophies and practices. It declared that African Environment Day would be celebrated jointly with Wangari Maathai Day on the third day of March annually in tribute to her contributions to the history, development, and politics of Kenya, Africa, and the international community (AU 2012, 1).

The AU's decision reads like a road map for the task of ensuring that Wangari Maathai's ideas and ideals are celebrated, preserved, and practically transmitted. The first three basis statements, which offer the rationale for the decision, create a profile of Maathai. The first claims her as a daughter of Africa while expressly noting that the impact of her work was global in nature. It also recognizes her contributions to the topical areas explored in chapters 2 to 5 of this book. The second statement lists her efforts toward human and environmental justice and notes her influence on the subjects covered in this book's chapters. Recognizing her commitment to what I have christened radical utu, the decision underscores in its second statement "Wangari Maathai's vision on protecting and promoting human well-being through her pioneering Green Belt Movement (GBM) and grass-roots activism, inspiring people to promote worldwide sustainable development" (AU 2012, 1). With its third statement, the decision qualified the regional and global significance and impact of Maathai's work, highlighting the fact that she had been the first African woman to receive a nod from the Norwegian Nobel Committee.

Against the foregoing validations, the AU presented the responsibilities of domestic and international actors in facilitating the decree of its decision. By so doing, it effectively contested the lamentable reduction of Maathai's work and profile outlined in the preface of this book. The statements of the AU's decision provide strategies for going beyond celebration to active dissemination of and interaction with Maathai's ideas and ideals in educational, cultural, political, and economic arenas, and so I use them to assess the state and extent of such engagement years after her passing. In statement number four, the AU welcomed "the ongoing international movement involving Governments, Civil Society Organizations, Regional and International Institutions to honor the value, vision, contribution and dedication of Wangari Maathai, thus inspiring people to call for human rights, peace and democracy, and environmental conservation" (AU 2012, 1). In this, the character of the movement envisioned by the AU is clear: it is global, inclusive, ongoing, and championed by institutions. A close study of the statements in the decision reveals three avenues the assembly considered through which to propagate Maathai's philosophies and practices. Along these, I structure the sections of this chapter: educational and scholarly engagement, institutional and individual activism, and memorialization initiatives.

Education and Scholarship

The AU's decision underscored the importance of bringing Maathai and her works and philosophies into educational institutions as deliberate curriculum and policy items. Statements eight and nine indicate that this can be achieved through teaching, research, policymaking, and supporting the Wangari Maathai Institute for Peace and Environmental Studies. In Statement eight, the AU encouraged "schools and universities to set up educational instruments and scholarship funds under the name of Wangari Maathai, to support students in the field of environment and sustainable development."

Many institutions of learning on the continent have initiatives to mark African Environment Day. Connecting the principles of that day more actively to the curriculum on an ongoing basis can boost efforts to embed environmental protection and sustainable development in institutional and societal cultures. Jessica Staudt, a fourth-grade teacher in Iowa, demonstrated the successful application of the Maathai principles in her classes. Her initiative allowed the children to interact with the worlds and words of Maathai, as Staudt and co-authors Erica M. Christie and Sarah E. Montgomery describe in their article "Little by Little: Global Citizenship through Local Action Inspired by Wangari Maathai" (Christie, Montgomery, and Staudt 2012). As one of her visions, Maathai maintained that in order to right the mishaps of the past, it was imperative to educate people as a corrective measure to ensure better and more sustainable practices for the future. To this end, she proposed prioritizing curricula that includes consciousness-raising for children from elementary to high school levels in order to develop utu-grounded individuals (Maathai 2009b, 232). Such curricula would include, in the teaching agenda, the imparting of values such as "justice, fairness, and accountability" to nurture conscientious leaders and citizens who could sustainably manage democracies and environments while innovating technologically (Maathai 2011a).

Institutions and individuals cultured in the practice of her models, she imagined, would actively embrace radical utu as a philosophy of life and not a one-off event. Maathai described this as manifesting in a number of ways, including a spirit of love for the environment (Maathai 2010, 90–91), gratitude and respect for the environment and others (108, 117–29), centering the needs of people in different communities, external empowerment and self-empowerment (131–41), self-knowledge (147), mindful and deliberate living (154–55), and commitment to service (157–58). My research indicates that while cocelebration of Wangari Maathai Day and Africa Environment Day ensures that some institutions explore her philosophies for that day, the prevailing challenge is the failure to sustain these values day to day.

Another challenge is the limiting conceptualization of her work as solely focused on the environment. The AU's decision emphasized sustainable development, which, as Maathai saw it, involved holistic approaches to meeting societies' needs and proper political, economic, and environmental management (Maathai 2009b, 2010, 2007a). She outlined the effect of this kind of holistic approach to sustainable development on societies and individuals in her Nobel Prize acceptance speech, saying, "In the process, the participants discover that they must be part of the solutions. They realize their hidden potential and are empowered to overcome inertia and take action. They come to recognize that they are the primary custodians and beneficiaries of the environment that sustains them" (2004c). Regrettably, many of the initiatives and projects instituted on Wangari Maathai Day/Africa Environment Day tend to focus solely on the environment, primarily tree planting, to the exclusion of other aspects of consciousness raising. Contributing to this state of affairs is a deficient knowledge of Maathai's principles and philosophies, a better understanding of which could enhance Wangari Maathai Day by helping to foster the institutional cultures and community values she advanced.

This limited acquaintance with Maathai's thoughts is due to the fact that Maathai the critical thinker is still only minimally explored, even by members of academic communities. Texts, articles, speeches, and interviews outlining her thoughts, which would serve as great resources for use at various levels of education, are still largely purchased or accessed by few individuals for personal reading. Thus, the information disseminated by educators and activists is often devoid of the layered depth of her assessments and insights. The analyses in the preceding chapters reveal a sophisticated thinker keen on critical interdisciplinary studies, and erasures of these nuances of her work compromise her profile as well as her ideas. The AU's vision—endorsing deliberate expansion of curricula to include studies on Maathai's ideas and ideals and financial investment in students and institutions—proposed to support the training of custodians of her legacy.

The AU further encouraged institutional support for the Wangari Maathai Institute for Peace and Environmental Studies, a constituent of University of Nairobi located in Kabete. WMI currently offers master's and doctoral degrees, and Maathai's values and principles inform the institute's academic, political, and social cultures. According to the its 2010–20 strategic plan, "WMI plans to institutionalize the experiences and values of Prof. Wangari Muta Maathai" (WMI 2010, 7). Jane Mutheu Mutune, a member of the first PhD cohort and currently a lecturer at WMI, explained, "Key to every interdisciplinary degree offered is environmental governance, incorporating the topical areas, democracy, cultures of peace, sustainability of livelihoods, and sustainable development" (interview with author, April 27, 2017). Professor Stephen Kiama, a former director of WMI, who was instrumental in its founding, adds that the institution, where Maathai served as the founding distinguished chair and the design of whose mission and academic culture she championed, honors her identity as a strong scholar and revolutionary thinker and actor (interview with author, July 12, 2018).

In its decision, the assembly encouraged the African Union Commission, within the framework of the Make Peace Happen Campaign, along with other stakeholders and partners, to take the necessary measures to back the development of WMI as an African Center of Excellence. The goal was to support the advancement of research on environmental governance and its linkages with peace, human rights, and democracy in Africa (WMI 2010, 2). Identified key partners included AU member states, private sector actors, the African Development Bank, UNEP, and other related international organizations and foundations in cooperation with the GBM. On this recommendation, a partnership between the African Development Bank, the University of Nairobi, and other organizations has ensured the expansion of WMI to a green campus, which opened in June 2019. The success of WMI and the accomplishment of this green project, conceptualized as carbon neutral and eventually autonomous in terms of its energy needs, demonstrates the usability of Maathai's ideas and ideals. Further acknowledgment of her contributions to knowledge creation is observable in the conferment of academic honors, including endowed chairs, and honorary doctorates during her lifetime and posthumously. Still, there is a glaring and puzzling scarcity of her ideas and philosophies within the classrooms of elementary schools, high schools, and universities, including some of those that endowed her with honors.

This deficit in curricula inclusion is matched in research and scholarship. Maathai is one of the most significant critical thinkers of our time, yet few scholars have rigorously studied her words that are on record in publications, speeches, and interviews. Maathai gave numerous public lectures and conference presentations and published articles and book chapters as well as the well-received books: *Replenishing the Earth: Spiritual Values for Healing Ourselves and the World* (2010); *The Challenge for Africa* (2009); *The Green Belt Movement: Sharing the Approach and the Experience* (2003); and her memoir, *Unbowed* (2007). Regrettably, these remain largely understudied and underused in research and teaching. Furthermore, few books have been written about her. Only one edited academic volume, *The Rhetorical Legacy of Wangari Maathai: Planting the Future* (2018), edited by Eddah M. Mutua, Alberto González, and Anke Wolbert, and one single-author, full-length book, *Wangari Maathai: Visionary, Environmental Leader, Political Activist* (2014) by Florence Namulunda, are in print. In the introduction to her book, Namulunda describes it, in part, as her "personal search for Maathai" (n.p.). Jean Estrada's e-publication, *Wangari Maathai: 57 Success Facts; Everything You Need to Know* (2014) is reductive right from its title. Fifty-seven things are certainly nowhere near everything there is to know about Maathai. Also, the very diminution of her profile to fifty-seven facts that are not contextualized is problematic, as is the assumption that the author has the power to define everything people need to know about her. Another equally subtractive booklet may also be considered an adult-age book on Maathai: *Women in African History: Wangari Maathai* by UNESCO (2015). The rest of a very limited assembly are mostly children's picture books: the sixteen-page *Wangari Maathai: Planting Trees for the Future* by Rebecca Allen (2006), *Wangari Maathai: The Woman Who Planted a Million Trees* by Franck Prévot (2015), *Mama Miti: Wangari Maathai and the Trees of Kenya* by Donna Jo Napoli (2012), *Seeds of Change:*

Planting a Path to Peace by Jen Cullerton Johnson (2010), *Wangari's Trees of Peace: A True Story from Africa* by Jeanette Winter (2008), and *Planting the Trees of Kenya: The Story of Wangari Maathai* by Claire Nivola (2008).

While there are a number of academic book chapters and articles (including Wambui 2018, Mutua and Omori 2018, Chirindo 2016, Wagner 2016, Hunt 2014, Presby 2013, Gorsevski 2012, and Nagel 2005) and a wide assortment of newspaper, magazine, and online articles on Wangari Maathai, in the area of published books, she and her philosophies appear to have been marketed more to the young. In the children's books, as is the case in other venues, her work with the environment is foregrounded to the exclusion of the rest of her advocacy and scholarly interests. The idea of training children to understand the need to protect the environment and perform as good citizens of the globe is necessary and valuable. Yet failure to educate adults who need to preserve natural as well as social and political environments does not support Maathai's contention that each generation has the responsibility to sustainably manage its environment so it can pass on a well-functioning world to the generations that follow. Educating adults becomes increasingly important in the midst of the prevailing debates on climate change, its effects, and its causative factors, especially those that are human-induced, such as fracking and deforestation. It is important to also note that directing Maathai's ideas principally at children also runs the risk of locating her as an unsophisticated thinker. Such a contracted narrative expunges the intricacies of a human being who, as the AU acknowledged, shaped historical events and impacted knowledge production. One hopes that this book's refocusing of the narrative to include her scholarly positions on a range of topics is a contribution to efforts toward easing the limiting concentration on her activism. Still, Professor Wangari Muta Maathai remains one of Africa's most recognized and celebrated activists, and it is equally important to explore the status of her legacy as an activist.

Activism

Maathai was a globally renowned activist. The AU acknowledged this in its decision in statement six, which mandated "the African Union (AU) Commission to take the necessary measures, together with Member States, for the observance of Wangari Maathai Day by the African Union," calling upon "all Member States, United Nations Agencies, and International and Civil Society Organizations, to actively observe Wangari Maathai Day." The implications of this dictate are clear. Member states living up to the spirit of the decision would ensure continued bearing of her activist ideals among their people in private and public institutions. In countries where citizens celebrated African Environment Day but were unfamiliar with Wangari Maathai, this provided an opportunity to spread her gospel of environmental justice, human rights, and sustainable development. Complying member states would conceivably share, and perhaps demand, these principles from foreign entities wishing to do business within their borders. Maathai advocated this kind of reestablishing of control and rebalancing globalization in proposing that African nations rewrite modalities of trade and interaction with their international partners to promote programs that support environmental and human rights protections (Maathai 1995a; 2009b, 111–14).

Maathai's stature as a public and global figure gave her capacity and influence matched by few to call attention to urgent issues for action. The AU's mandate provided a platform through which, in her absence, institutions and individuals at continental and global levels could enduringly execute these conversations and activist initiatives. In the following paragraphs, I inquire into the propagation of three of Maathai's principles on activism that emerged in this book: activism is a way of life not an event, activist concerns are interrelated and so solutions must be holistic, and radical utu.

Per the first of these principles, if activism is a way of life, then effective and sustainable activism is ongoing practice. Many institutions observe African Environment Day/Wangari Maathai Day and then make no further investment in yearlong commitments or projects toward green living or greening environments. This turns their environmental conservation and other activism into performances of activism or activist theater, not committed advocacy. Sustained cultures of activism require institutional buy-in, including from instruments of governments. This can help nurture individual activists while providing structures within which such individuals can direct their own activist efforts (Maathai 2009a). Maathai advocated for sustainable individual acts of activism as a lifestyle and life principle (Maathai 2010b, 107, 114; 2009d; 2004a). This is epitomized in the Be a Hummingbird movement. She often told the story of the hummingbird

(2010b). The hummingbird movement fosters self-declared ambassadors and champions for bettering the world. The GBM has published on its website a plan for how one can get involved in this movement with nothing more than good will and commitment to change (GBM, n.d.). "I will be a hummingbird" has become a rallying cry and motivational quote for people seeking to help realize change in their societies as their way of being and designing their personal activist plans and philosophies. The movement, boosted by social media sharing by individuals across the world of their hummingbird narratives and pledges, continues to grow.

A similar movement inspired by Maathai, My Little Thing, has followed the same developmental pattern as the hummingbird movement. Maathai famously stated, "It's the little things citizens do. That's what will make the difference. My little thing is planting trees" (Wangari Maathai Foundation n.d.). Launched by the Wangari Maathai Foundation as a social media campaign, #mylittlething, and famously popularized by talk show host Oprah Winfrey, My Little Thing quickly became a global movement of inspiration to people from different walks of life (KTN News 2015).[1]

The second principle of Maathai's brand of activism proposes that different societal challenges are interrelated and interdependent and thus require holistic activist approaches to resolve. For this reason, different activist movements need to inform and feed off each other and consolidate efforts in processes of erecting and maintaining functioning communities. Environmental conservation, for example, is inextricably linked to other societal concerns, including human rights, peace and/or conflict, gender issues, food security, health, and democracy. In her Nobel Prize acceptance speech, Maathai shared the significance of the GBM method, which helped people "make connections between their own personal actions and the problems they witness in the environment and in society. They learn that our world is confronted with a litany of woes: corruption, violence against women and children, disruption and breakdown of families, and disintegration of cultures and communities" (2004c). Managing such interrelated complexities demands activism that is holistic and people driven. Holistic activism by its nature is inclusive because it calls for participation of people from different demographics and with different experiences and competencies. By focusing primarily on tree planting, many celebrations of African Environment Day/ Wangari Maathai Day and other activist endeavors fail to embrace the significance of the interconnectedness of the issues, an elaboration that would bring more people to the activist table. Inclusiveness ensures that more segments of society are connected and involved, a necessary ingredient in realizing well-functioning and democratic communities. It is undeniably important to celebrate Maathai as a way to continue and expand her vision and mission, but in doing so it is necessary to ensure the completeness of the message and ideas conveyed within that commemoration.

A third principle of Maathai's activist philosophy is that utu-respecting communities are intrinsically activist, and so a spirit of utu is necessary to create and raise activist communities and societies. Utu-directed living is indeed always a daily exercise in change making. The reality of individuals picking up the banner of protecting the environment and human rights, as Maathai noted on multiple occasions, is important; it is perhaps the most essential principle to creating functioning communities. However, with governments, civil society, global bodies, and educational and other institutions failing to play their part as outlined in the AU mandate, the efforts of scattered individuals have a minimized impact. This is especially so if those countermanding the work of the individuals are the very institutions that should offer systems under which such industry can thrive. For example, environmental protection remains addressed mostly through lip service by many governments in Africa, resulting in continued abuse of natural resources, decline of natural ecosystems, and increase in drought, famine, and poverty in large parts of the continent (Maathai 1995a, 2007a, 2009b). The challenge necessitates institutions and communities creating policies toward environmental and climate justice and protections for human rights and democratic spaces to preserve cultures of activism and radical utu in all its forms.

The AU, through the invitation to allies to institutionalize Maathai's activist principles, aspired to activate regional and global activist communities. Maathai offered blueprints for creating activist communities and movements with global influence like the ones the AU envisioned. The biggest movements she inspired, which showcase these principles, continue to regenerate and produce efforts and participants across the continents. The most identifiable of these is the GBM, which Marc Michaelson, in discussing the creation of movements (1994), designates as a consensus movement. Kathleen Hunt, in "'It's More Than Planting Trees, It's Planting Ideas': Ecofeminist Praxis in the Green Belt Movement" (2014), highlights the social change potential of the principles of the GBM. The movement continues its operations and maintains a global presence with an international board and offices in the United States and the United Kingdom. The GBM's board chair, Wanjira Mathai, wrote in its 2015 annual report, "The Movement provided training to over 200 rural women and community-based organizations who have in turn trained over 20,000 members of their communities in natural resource management and impacted thousands of others" (GBM 2016, 3).

Another global movement Wangari Maathai inspired, and that also demonstrates her activist principles, was the Billion Tree Campaign. In 2006, UNEP, with collaborators in Nairobi, launched the campaign with the goal of planting at least one billion trees worldwide annually. In 2011, the Plant-for-the-Planet foundation took over the project, which carries forward Maathai's commitment of planting indigenous trees to protect biodiversity and fragile ecosystems. As of January 2018, the project, which raises environmental warriors and warrior collectives, had far surpassed the target of one billion trees a year (Plant-for-the-Planet n.d.).

Because Maathai's ideas and ideals on activism adopt the performance of utu as both the process and end goal, they are easily translatable and importable to different demographics and geographies. It is this that feeds the people-driven nature of the movements she has inspired. Therefore, they hold value for activist initiatives as well as research and classroom experiences across the disciplines on environmental, social and political justice, and human rights. Maathai's profile as an activist has been broadcast more than her scholarship, and because of that, her activist legacy appears to have been better safeguarded, thus far, than her scholarly one. Scholarly research on Maathai's activism can help secure the continuation of her activist legacy, and the resulting perpetuated activist traditions can enrich scholarly research on Maathai and social justice in general. The practice of Maathai's brand of activism continually memorializes her as much as the deliberate memorialization efforts by institutions covered in the next section.

Memorializing Initiatives

Institutions best serve sustained memory because while personal memories can die with individuals, institutional and community memories survive generations. To capture the substantial implications of the recommendations in action statements seven, eight, and ten by the Assembly of the AU, it is important to note that the earlier described minimal engagement with Maathai's work in teaching and scholarship is indicative of the larger ill of writing women out of history as well as the erasure of African thinkers from the academy and scholarship. The AU's decision, therefore, addressed this erasure from history of African and women achievers. This section surveys institutional memorialization of Maathai, her ideas, and her ideals in geographic and virtual landscapes as well as through the institution of awards, as proposed by the AU's decision.

The AU urged "Member States to name public landmarks including streets, parks, squares, schools and institutes of peace in universities and other national monuments after Wangari Maathai, as a way to memorialize her life's work and serve as a tribute to inspire current and future generations to preserve the planet" (AU 2012, 1). Geographic memorializing marks those christening public and private spaces and monuments in her honor as claiming a stake in Maathai's value and idea systems. Such public celebration impacts institutions and individuals, as pronounced in the following statement by Stephen D. Minnis, president of Maathai's alma mater, Benedictine College (formerly Mount St. Scholastica): "To have a statue of Wangari Maathai on our campus has been a dream for a while, and it is appropriate that it is here in St. Scholastica Plaza, where our students will see it and aspire to be like her" (*Atchinson Globe* 2014). He made this statement at the June 2014 installation of the Wangari Maathai statue at the university by her graduating cohort from 1964 at their class reunion. Prior to this, a tree had been planted in St. Scholastica Plaza in her honor. In 2013, her other alma mater, the University of Pittsburgh, dedicated the Wangari Maathai Trees and Garden (University of Pittsburgh 2013). At the University of Florida, the African Studies Center has dedicated a Wangari Maathai tree and bench. Other gardens and parks that have been named for Wangari Maathai include Wangari Gardens in Washington, DC (Wangari Gardens n.d.); the Wangari Maathai Natural Garden at the Al Raby School for Community and Environment in Chicago; the Wangari Maathai Park in Lima, Peru; and, fittingly, a garden at the AU headquarters in Addis Ababa. While institutions on the continent of Africa have been slow to hearken to the AU's call, others across the world have stepped up to the plate.

In Kenya, not enough effort has been directed at keeping Maathai alive in public memory. One significant undertaking, however, was the 2016 renaming of Nairobi's Forest Road to Professor Wangari Maathai Road. At a private level, efforts through the Wangari Maathai Foundation are in progress to establish the Wangari Muta Maathai House, a legacy project. The project's concept paper envisions a place that represents the values held by Maathai, which will serve as inspiration for visitors to embrace her ways of being and knowing. The foundation's website declares that the project purposes to "instill the conviction that everyone can be a force for positive change with commitment, persistence and patience by celebrating the life and work of Wangari Maathai" (GBM 2013, 6–7). Brookhouse School in Karen, Nairobi, has dedicated the Wangari Maathai Sixth Form Center, comprising a building and small garden.

With technological and technologically motivated lifestyle changes, the virtual landscape has become increasingly central to education, economics, politics, and the socialization of individuals and societies. It is therefore noteworthy that digital platforms have delivered key constituents of those memorializing Maathai. Individuals continue to utilize these spaces to celebrate, historicize, quote, or critique her. On April 1, 2013, marking what would have been Maathai's seventy-third birthday, Google honored her with a doodle on its homepage. Such digital institutions actively introduce Maathai to new demographics across the globe.

Also introducing Maathai's values and critical thoughts to new audiences are awards instated in her honor. Awards allow for continued collective memory, as those presenting the award, those feted, those striving to receive the awards, and those watching and celebrating inescapably are present to the ideologies the award symbolizes. As part of the AU's decision, the the continental Wangari Maathai Award for Outstanding African Achievements in Environment and Biodiversity Conservation was established to pay tribute to individuals' achievements in protecting the environment (AU 2012, 2). Other organizations have followed the lead of the AU. In 2012, the Collaborative Partnership on Forests established the Wangari Maathai Forest Champion Award with a cash prize of twenty thousand dollars to recognize efforts and contributions to forest and environmental management and preservation. Benedictine College endowed the Maathai Discovery Award to support student projects "that focus on stewardship, sustainability, women's equality, and/or environmental justice" (Benedictine College n.d.). Presented annually to recognized high school seniors in the New York City public school system, the Wangari Maathai Award for Civic Participation in Sustainability is an annual ten-thousand-dollar cash prize, supported by the Rockefeller Foundation, the Bette Midler Family Trust, and the New York City Department of Parks and Recreation and managed by the Municipal Art Society of New York (MAS n.d.). These awards endowed in her name, like those that were bequeathed to Maathai, as she stated, also bring "international attention to our efforts" (Maathai 2007a, 178). In the arenas of academia and research, the Africa Conference hosted annually at the University of Texas at Austin established in 2016 the Wangari Maathai Award for Innovative Scholarship and Leadership to celebrate the work of an emerging junior scholar whose work has the potential to be transformational. In South Africa, the Wangari Maathai Impact Award, inaugurated in 2018 by Deep Learning Indaba, recognizes work by African innovators in the areas of machine learning and artificial intelligence.

The AU, with its 2012 decision, sought to encourage the preservation, dissemination, and application of Wangari Maathai's critical thoughts, philosophies, and practices. There is reason to celebrate the fact that the passing on of her ideas and ideals is sustained to a significant extent by individuals, which is very much in line with Maathai's conviction that "entire communities also come to understand that while it is necessary to hold their governments accountable, it is equally important that in their own relationships with each other, they exemplify the leadership values they wish to see in their own leaders, namely justice, integrity and trust" (Maathai 2004c). Still, it bears noting that the AU's call to "governments, civil society organizations, regional and international institutions" remains largely unattended to. While Maathai encouraged ownership of ideas by individuals as foundational to the creation of movements and grounded communities, the lack of extended buy-in that the AU hoped for from institutions means that some potential positive effects of promoting Maathai's ideas and ideals are forfeited. The individuals' efforts would be served and enhanced by institutional capacities that lend credibility and logistical support, facilitate the creation of operational cultures in societies and institutions, and legitimate values and practices.

The foregoing and the deliberations in the other chapters indicate the persistence of the areas of concern that Wangari Maathai championed and the challenges she fought to resolve. I have mined her words and life's narrative to establish her core ideas and principles on selected topics and then delineated from these, philosophies, models, and theories. I have noted that the limited recording of the potential global impact of her critical thoughts has been one of the failures of the activist and academic communities. This and other oversights exposed in this chapter have contributed to the lessening of Maathai's profile identified in the preface of this book and her ideas and ideals discussed in its chapters. I have offered frameworks and language for accessing her critical thoughts and values. My hope is that such definition furnishes scholars, institutions, activists, and other individuals with clear tasks to engage, question, contest, and test. Further, it should inform the continuation of her work, including in areas in which she had an interest but ran out of time to complete, specifically violence against girls and women and HIV/AIDS interventions. In considering the motivation and purpose for carrying on her work, it is important to remember that her entire body of work, as illustrated by this book, was about building strong, well-functioning communities and systems rooted in radical utu at all levels. This is the legacy of Wangari Muta Maathai.

Appendix 1

Awards and Honors

Including in this book a record of Wangari Muta Maaathai's awards, honors, and service positions is strategic, allowing documentation of a part of her narrative left uncovered by the preceding chapters. They have offered insight into her critical ideas and activities as a scholar activist, but it is difficult to appreciate the extent of her influence globally without considering her awards and service.

The Norwegian Nobel Committee, whose press release on October 8, 2004, announcing Maathai's Nobel Peace Prize cited her holistic approach to sustainable development that respects human and environmental justice, was not alone in registering its respect for her work and philosophies. She received the highest civilian honors in two countries and honors from government bodies on three continents. From the French Republic in 2016, she was received into the Legion of Honor. In her own country, the government of Kenya, whose representatives at certain points had labeled her an enemy of the state, honored her as an elder of the Order of the Burning Spear in 2003 and as an elder of the Order of the Golden Heart in 2004. She was received into the Grand Cordon of the Order of the Rising Sun of Japan in 2009 and the Order of the Golden Ark in the Netherlands in 1994.

Influential global institutions equally heavily endorsed the significance of Maathai's activist and scholarly efforts. In 2005, *Time* magazine named her one of the hundred most influential people in the world, and she made it into *Forbes* magazine's list of the one hundred most powerful women in the world (*Forbes* 2005). She was also ranked sixth in the peer review of the world's "Top 100 Eco-Heroes" by the United Kingdom's Environment Agency. In 1991, she made it into UNEP's Global 500 Hall of Fame and was named one of the hundred heroines of the world. *Earth Times* named her one of the top one hundred people in the world making a difference in environmental matters. In 1995, Maathai was inducted into the International Women's Hall of Fame by the International Women's Forum Leadership Foundation, which every year "inducts one or more of the world's leading female pioneers" (IWF). The rest of this appendix showcases other awards and honors.

Awards

Vanderbilt University, Nichols-Chancellor's Medal, 2011
NAACP Image Award–Chairman's Award, 2009
Elizabeth Blackwell Award, Hobart and William Smith Colleges, 2008
Girl Guides and Girl Scouts World Citizenship Award, 2007
Livingstone Medal, Royal Scottish Geographical Society, 2007
Nelson Mandela Award for Health and Human Rights, Henry J. Kaiser
    Family Foundation, 2007
Cross of the Order of St. Benedict, Benedictine College, 2007
Indira Gandhi Prize for Peace, Disarmament and Development, Indira
    Gandhi Memorial Trust, 2006
Lifetime Achievement Award, Kenya National Commission on Human
    Rights, 2006
UCI Citizen Peacebuilding Award, Irvine Center for Citizen Peacebuild-
    ing, University of California, Irvine, 2006
Sophie Prize (for contributions to environmental and sustainable devel-
    opment), 2004
Petra Kelly Prize (for contributions to protection of the environment and
    human rights), 2004
J. Sterling Morton Award, Arbor Day Foundation, 2004
Conservation Scientist Award, Columbia University, 2004
Global Environment Award, World Association of Non-Governmental
    Organizations, 2003
Outstanding Vision and Commitment Award, Bridges to Community of
    Canada, 2002
Juliet Hollister Award (for embracing interfaith philosophies and prac-
    tices), Temple of Understanding, 2001
Excellence Award, Kenya Community Abroad, 2001
Jane Addams Leadership Award, Jane Addams Conference, 1993

Edinburgh Medal, Medical Research Council, United Kingdom, 1993
Africa Prize for Leadership, Hunger Project, 1991
Goldman Environmental Prize, Goldman Foundation, 1991
Offeramus Medal, Benedictine College, 1990
Woman of the World Award, WomanAid, United Kingdom (alongside
  Mother Theresa), 1989
Windstar Award (founded by John Denver for environmental work), 1988
Medal, Better World Society, 1986
Right Livelihood Award (a.k.a. the Alternative Nobel Prize), 1984
Woman of the Year, 1983

Advocacies and Committees

Cofounder/member, Laureate Women's Initiative
Inaugural presiding officer, African Union's Economic, Social and Cul-
  tural Council, 2005
Cofounder (with UNEP), Billion Tree Campaign, 2005
Cochair (with Paul Martin), Congo Basin Forest Fund, 2007–11
Goodwill ambassador, Project to Save the Congo Basin Forest Ecosys-
  tem, 2005–11

Policy, Advisory, and Executive Boards Service

Commission on the Future
Democracy Coalition Project
Earth Charter Commission
Environment Liaison Center International
Global Crop Diversity Trust
Green Cross International
Human Rights Watch Women's Rights Project
Jane Goodall Institute
Millennium Development Goals Advocacy Group
National Council of Women of Kenya
Prince Albert II of Monaco Foundation
United Nations Commission on Global Governance
United Nations Secretary-General's Advisory Board on Disarmament
Women and Environment Development Organization
World Learning for International Development
WorldWIDE Network of Women in Environmental Work, USA

Patron

Billion Tree Campaign
Congo Basin Forest Fund
Mottainai Campaign, Japan

Academic Honors: Endowed Chairs and Honorary Degrees

Doctor of Science (posthumous)	Syracuse University, USA	2013
Doctor of Agriculture	University of Copenhagen	2010
Doctorate Degree	Kwansei Gakuin University, Japan	2010
Doctor of Humane Letters	Meredith College, USA	2009
Doctor of Science	Egerton University, Kenya	2007
Doctor of Public Service Honoris Causa	University of Pittsburgh, USA	2006
Doctor of Humane Letters	Connecticut College, USA	2006
Doctor of Science	Morehouse College, USA	2006
Doctor of Science	Ochanomizu University, Japan	2005
Doctor of Science	Willamette University, USA	2005
Doctor of Science	University of Nairobi, Kenya	2005
Doctor of Science	Soka University, Japan	2004
Doctor of Science	Aoyama Gakuin University, Japan	2004
Doctor of Law	Yale University, USA	2004
Endowed Chair in Gender and Women's Studies named "Fuller-Maathai"	Connecticut College, USA	2000
Doctor of Agriculture	University of Norway	1997
Doctor of Science	Hobart and William Smith Colleges, USA	1994
Doctor of Law	Williams College, USA	1990

Appendix 2

Saving Karura

Just as the GBM started planting solely indigenous trees in 1998, Wangari Maathai and others were embroiled in protests against the privatization of Karura, an indigenous urban forest in Nairobi, gazetted in 1932. Her efforts and struggles attached to the saving of the forest would lead to *Time* magazine naming her Hero of the Week in December 1998.

Toward the end of 1998, some members of the Kenyan government had started allocating sections of Karura Forest to individuals for private development, drawing widespread outrage. Even the Architectural Association of Kenya cautioned its members against participating in any work that would contribute to the destruction of the forest. The urgency to save Karura was exacerbated by the drought that plagued the region at the end of the 1990s, leading to starvation in some parts by the year 2000. On October 7, 1998, Maathai accompanied opposition MPs and other activists on a tree-planting mission in parts of the forest already cleared for development. The event's activities are reported to have escalated into the destruction and burning of hundreds of thousands of dollars' worth of construction equipment in the forest.

On January 8, 1999, Maathai was once again embroiled in a physical confrontation with representatives of the government. While attempting to plant trees in the forest, she and twenty others, including opposition MPs, two German environmentalists, and journalists, were attacked and prevented from entering the forest by a reported group of about two hundred men under orders to stand guard. Maathai was injured and taken to Nairobi Hospital for treatment.

While police declined to act on her report, video footage from the attack triggered local and global criticism and fury, and the attorney general apologized to Maathai, promising an inquiry into the incident. On January 11, 1999, Amnesty International released the public statement "Ill-Treatment / Fear for Safety" on Wangari Maathai's situation. The communiqué urged that appeals for the protection of Maathai and Karura Forest be sent to Maj. Marsden Madoka, then Minister of State in the Office of the President, and to Commissioner of Police Duncan Wachira and copied to Attorney General Amos Wako, Minister for Natural Resources Francis Lotodo, and the media. The UN secretary-general, Kofi Annan, and other world leaders also condemned the attack on Maathai and her supporters.

This incident aggravated already present ire about the grabbing of Karura Forest and other public property, prompting protests that would last for weeks. From the end of January to the beginning of February, students at Kenyatta University and the University of Nairobi demonstrated against the Karura plans. On January 30, they marched to Karura to plant trees, and when government forces responded with violence, riots broke out across the city, leading to the temporary closure of the universities. The government defended the project, ordering the arrest of opposition MPs Njehu Gatabaki, James Orengo, and David Mwenje, whom it denounced for participating in the student protests.

Global indignation at the Kenyan government grew. Klaus Töpfer, the executive director of UNEP, stated that the organization would consider moving its headquarters out of Kenya if harm came to Karura Forest. He also vowed that UNEP staff would continue to water the Meru oak tree that Maathai had led women in planting at the UNEP compound gate after Chief Inspector Paul Muluma and his team of armed riot police, who blocked their entry into the forest, had stopped them from planting at the gate of Karura Forest. The protests ended only when the president announced that he was instituting a ban on the allocation of public land. The plans for Karura, which had included a golf course and a high-end housing estate, were thus thwarted, although some questions remained about the destruction of equipment at the October 1998 protest event. While Maathai claimed that the vigilantes guarding the forest had destroyed the equipment because of gripes about poor payment, others, including President Moi, argued that her supporters had in fact gotten out of control and burned the equipment.

Karura Forest Reserve is today home to over six hundred wildlife species, including mammals, reptiles, birds, and butterflies. Over one-third of its acreage is covered by indigenous trees. The scenic forest has rivers, waterfalls, and caves as well as walking trails for hikers and exercisers. Other popular activities in the park include forest drives, bird and butterfly watching, cycling, and picnicking (Kenya Forest Service n.d.).

Notes

Preface

1. The use of the generalizing terms "Africa" and "African" in many segments of the book and in analysis is necessary because it accurately represents Maathai's use of the words in those instances. It is also for ease of communication.

Chapter 1: Birthing Radical Selves

1. An affiliate of the University of Nairobi, WMI is housed on a green/sustainable campus in Kabete. The WMI Project Architectural and Land Use Plan Brief explains that the institute was "established to honor, recognize, celebrate, advance, and immortalize the ideals and works of . . . the 2004 Peace Nobel Laureate, Prof. Wangari Muta Maathai. Thus, the institute will promote good environmental practices and cultivate cultures of peace by shaping values, ethics and attitudes of its graduates through experiential learning, mentoring and transformational leadership" (WMI n.d.). WMI fosters holistic cross-disciplinary and multidisciplinary research, and students earn interdisciplinary master's and doctoral degrees. The institute also offers a variety of short courses. To meet its commitment to community engagement and experiential research and pedagogy, WMI has established demonstration farms and partnerships with institutions in Kenya and across the globe. WMI serves "university students, researchers, policy makers, the private sector, community leaders and groups interested in good practices in environmental management and peace building" (WMI n.d.).

2. Professor Stephen Gitahi Kiama was the first director of WMI (2010–16), intermittently acting principal of the College of Agriculture and Veterinary Sciences (2004–15), and the principal of the College of Agriculture and Veterinary Sciences from 2016.

Chapter 3: Eco-agency and Unbowed Personhood

1. *Harambee*, a Swahili word, refers to pulling together or pooling efforts. The word, an official motto of Kenya, appears on the nation's coat of arms. The country's first leader adopted the motto as foundational to the building of the new nation following independence, rallying individuals and communities to work together.

2. Waiyaki wa Hinga.

Chapter 4: Theorizing and Activating Utu Citizenships

1. The six were Agnes Ndetei, Phoebe Asiyo, Charity Ngilu, Nyiva Mwendwa, Mary Wanjiru Mwangi, and Martha Karua.

2. An angry opposition condemned the move as illegal and intended to undercut the opposition's zealous parliamentary agenda, particularly its plan to debate Moi's fourteen-year leadership and ethnic violence in the country.

Chapter 5: Just Globalization

1. Maathai specified, "If African states' agricultural extension services had not been underfunded or neglected in the decades since African nations became independent, this farmer not only might have learned the right way to prepare the soil for planting, she also might have had access to information, modern equipment, and governmental support that would have enabled her to farm more efficiently and less destructively" (2009b, 17).

2. Purchased by Bayer AG in 2018, Monsanto was a multinational American corporation that was founded as a chemical company and advanced into the production of genetically modified seeds/organisms, artificial sweeteners, and a wide variety of other products. It developed a near monopoly in the seed-production area, disrupting environments and gaining significant control over food production in many markets. Due to the danger of some of its products and policies to environments and populations, Monsanto was accused of ecocide. Maathai's arguments on Monsanto are applicable to companies such as Cargill, Evogene, DowDuPont, and others that have been involved in the production of agricultural chemicals and genetically modified organisms and participated in practices that disadvantage some populations across the world.

3. Maathai offered an example in her Nobel Prize acceptance lecture, stating, "Women did not realize that meeting their needs depended on their environment being healthy and well managed. They were also unaware that a degraded environment leads to a scramble for scarce resources and may culminate in poverty and even conflict. They were also unaware of the injustices of international economic arrangements" (2004c).

4. In her 2005 Nelson Mandela Lecture "Rise Up and Walk!," Maathai said, "One of the constraints, even for the government, is that we have not invested enough in education and especially in technical education. Technical education would give citizens knowledge, skills and experience, which would make them competent, confident and competitive. Such personnel would create opportunities for entrepreneurship and wealth creation" (2005d).

5. Maathai argued, "Only a new partnership in a new era of cooperation could make government and its people agree to transfer technological information which can make a difference. With such new partnership and international cooperation, local innovations and initiatives would be supported without discrimination" (1995a).

Chapter 6: Scholar-Activist Legacy

1. Established in 2015, the Wangari Maathai Foundation is a legacy project honoring the scholar-activist. The foundation seeks to encourage people's activation and promotion of "the vision of Prof. Wangari Maathai by engaging in and supporting activities that inspire them to live lives of purpose, committed to integrity and courageous leadership" (Wangari Maathai Foundation n.d.). More details on the foundation, the Wangari Muta Maathai House, and other projects can be found at http://www.wangarimaathai.org.

References

Allen, Chris. 1997. "Who Needs Civil Society?" *Review of African Political Economy* 24 (73): 329–37.

Allen, Rebecca. 2006. *Wangari Maathai: Planting Trees for the Future.* Boston: Houghton Mifflin Harcourt.

Amadiume, Ifi. 1997. *Re-inventing Africa: Matriarchy, Religion and Culture.* London: Zed Books.

Amnesty International. 1993. "Fear for Safety: KENYA; Wangari Maathai (female)—Environmentalist, Opposition Activist." Accessed July, 13 2015. https://www.amnesty.org/download/Documents/188000/afr320071993en .pdf.

Atchison Globe. 2014. "Nobel Peace Winner Immortalized with Statue at Benedictine College." Atchison Globe Now. June 25, 2014. http://www .atchisonglobenow.com/community_and_lifestyles/good_news _atchison/nobel-peace-winner-immortalized-with-statue-at-benedictine -college/article_ae5c3ce9-040b-5161-97d7-1d424c5b9e03.html.

AU (African Union). 2012. "Decision Recognizing the Life and Work of Wangari Muta Maathai (Doc. Assembly/AU/14(XVIII) Add.6)." https://archives.au.int/bitstream/handle/123456789/1320/Assembly %20AU%20Dec%20406%20%28XVIII%29%20_E.pdf?sequence =1&isAllowed=y.

Benedictine College. n.d. "Wangari Maathai Day: March 3." https://www .benedictine.edu/about/notable-alumni/wangari-maathai.

Berkes, Fikret, and Mina Kislalioglu Berkes. 2009. "Ecological Complexity, Fuzzy Logic, and Holism in Indigenous Knowledge." *Futures* 41 (1): 6–12.

Branch, Daniel. 2007. "The Enemy Within: Loyalists and the War against Mau Mau in Kenya." *Journal of African History* 48 (2): 291–315.

———. 2010. "The Search for the Remains of Dedan Kimathi: The Politics of Death and Memorialization in Post-Colonial Kenya." *Past and Present* 206 (suppl. 5): 301–20.

Chegu, Fatuma, and Sheila P. Wamahiu. 1999. "Empowering Strategy for Dealing with Sexual Harassment and Abuse: A Case Study from Kenya." In *Women, Education and Empowerment*, edited by Digumarti Bhaskara Rao and Digumarti Pushpalatha Rao, 415–23. New Delhi: Discovery Publishing House.

Chirindo, Kundai. 2016. "Bantu Sociolinguistics in Wangari Maathai's Peacebuilding Rhetoric." *Women's Studies in Communication* 39 (4): 442–59.

Christie, Erica, Sarah Montgomery, and Jessica Staudt. 2012. "Little by Little: Global Citizenship through Local Action Inspired by Wangari Maathai." *Social Studies and the Young Learner* 25 (2): 8–11.

Collins, Carole. 1999. "Break the Chains of Debt! International Jubilee 2000 Campaign Demands Deeper Debt Relief." *Review of African Political Economy* 26 (81): 419–22.

Dalby, Alexa. 2011. "Wangari Maathai a Force of Nature." Free Library. November 1, 2011. https://www.thefreelibrary.com/Wangari%20Maathai%20a%20force%20of%20nature.-a0272895282.

Dlova, Ncoza, Saja H. Hamed, Joyce Tsoka-Gwegweni, Anneke Grobler, and Richard Hift. 2014. "Women's Perceptions of the Benefits and Risks of Skin-Lightening Creams in Two South African Communities." *Journal of Cosmetic Dermatology* 13 (3): 236–41.

Duke, Lynne. 2004. "From the Ground Up: Wangari Maathai's Plan for Cultivating Peace Is Taking Root in Africa." *Washington Post*, December 26, 2004. http://www.washingtonpost.com/wp-dyn/articles/A24008-2004Dec24.html.

Elkins, Caroline. 2000. "The Struggle for Mau Mau Rehabilitation in Late Colonial Kenya." *International Journal of African Historical Studies* 33 (1): 25–57.

Estrada, Jean. 2014. *Wangari Maathai: 57 Success Facts; Everything You Need to Know*. Apsley, Australia: Emereo Publishing.

Forbes. 2005. "#68 Wangari Maathai." The 100 Most Powerful Women. Forbes.com. https://www.forbes.com/lists/2005/11/BDLL.html.

Fox, Roddy. 1996. "Bleak Future for Multi-Party Elections in Kenya." *Journal of Modern African Studies* 34 (4): 597–607.

GBM (Green Belt Movement). 2013. "A Legacy Project: The Wangari Muta Maathai House." http://www.greenbeltmovement.org/sites/greenbeltmovement.org/files/Wangari%20Maathai%20House%20Concept%20Note.pdf#overlay-context=node/699.

———. 2016. *Annual Report 2015*. http://www.greenbeltmovement.org/sites/greenbeltmovement.org/files/GBM%202015%20Annual%20Report.pdf.

———. n.d. "Condolences from World Leaders and Friends." Accessed April 16, 2016. http://www.greenbeltmovement.org/node/307.

Githuku, Nicholas K. 2015. *Mau Mau Crucible of War: Statehood, National Identity, and Politics of Postcolonial Kenya*. Lanham, MD: Lexington Books.

Gorsevski, Ellen W. 2012. "Wangari Maathai's Emplaced Rhetoric: Greening Global Peacebuilding." *Environmental Communication: A Journal of Nature and Culture* 6 (3): 290–307.

————. 2018. "Growing the Next Generation: The Sustainability of Wangari Maathai's Rhetoric of Environmentalism." In Mutua, González, and Wolbert, *Rhetorical Legacy of Wangari Maathai*, 171–88.

Hansen, Benno. 2011. "Wangari Maathai Honorary Doctorate Lecture." Copenhagen University. Vimeo. https://vimeo.com/26104320.

Headey, Derek, and Christopher B. Barrett. 2015. "Opinion: Measuring Development Resilience in the World's Poorest Countries." *Proceedings of the National Academy of Sciences* 112 (37): 11423–25.

Heather, Randall W. 2017. "Intelligence and Counter-Insurgency in Kenya, 1952–56." In *Modern Counter-Insurgency*, edited by Ian Beckett, 77–105. New York: Routledge.

Home, Robert. 2012. "Colonial Township Laws and Urban Governance in Kenya." *Journal of African Law* 56 (2): 175–93.

Hunt, Kathleen P. 2014. "'It's More Than Planting Trees, It's Planting Ideas': Ecofeminist Praxis in the Green Belt Movement." *Southern Communication Journal* 79 (3): 235–49.

IWF (International Women's Forum). n.d. International Hall of Fame. https://www.iwforum.org/international_hall_of_fame.

Kanogo, Tabitha. 1987. *Squatters and the Roots of Mau Mau, 1905–63*. London: Currey.

Kanyinga, Karuti. 2009. "The Legacy of the White Highlands: Land Rights, Ethnicity and the Post-2007 Election Violence in Kenya." *Journal of Contemporary African Studies* 27 (3): 325–44.

Kanyinga, Karuti, and James D. Long. 2012. "The Political Economy of Reforms in Kenya: The Post-2007 Election Violence and a New Constitution." *African Studies Review* 55 (1): 31–51.

Kennedy, Kerry, and Nan Richardson, eds. 2004. *Speak Truth to Power: Human Rights Defenders Who Are Changing Our World*. Photographs by Eddie Adams. New York: Crown.

Kenya Forest Service. n.d. "Karura Forest." http://www.kenyaforestservice.org/index.php?option=com_content&view=article&id=77&Itemid=523.

Kitetu, Catherine. 2013. "Organisational Networks of Kenyan Female Migrants in England: The Humble Chama Now Operating at Higher International Levels." Retrieved from codesria.org.

Koster, Mickie Mwanzia. 2014. "Mau Mau Inventions and Reinventions." In *Contemporary Africa*, edited by Toyin Falola and Emmanuel Mbah, 23–45. New York: Palgrave Macmillan.

————. 2016. *The Power of the Oath: Mau Mau Nationalism in Kenya, 1952–1960*. Rochester, NY: University of Rochester Press.

Kramon, Eric, and Daniel N. Posner. 2011. "Kenya's New Constitution." *Journal of Democracy* 22 (2): 89–103.

KTN News. 2015. "#MyLittleThing: Remembering Wangari Maathai—What Is Your Little Thing?" YouTube. September 18, 2015. https://www.youtube.com/watch?v=QzIKx98P8jE.

Kushner, Jennifer Lara Simka. 2009. "Righteous Commitment: Renewing, Repairing, and Restoring the World—Wangari Maathai and the Green Belt Movement." PhD diss., National-Louis University, March 2009. https://digitalcommons.nl.edu/diss/23.

Maathai, Wangari. 1994. *The Bottom Is Heavy Too: Even with the Green Belt Movement*. Fifth Edinburgh Medal Address. Edinburgh: Edinburgh University Press.

———. 1995a. "Bottlenecks to Development in Africa." Speech, Fourth UN World Women's Conference, Beijing, August 30, 1995.

———. 1995b. "Women, Information, and the Future: The Women of Kenya and the Green Belt Movement." In *A Rising Public Voice: Women in Politics Worldwide*, 241–50, edited by Alida Brill. New York: Feminist Press at the City University of New York.

———. 2000. "Women and the Environment." In Kennedy and Richardson, *Speak Truth to Power*, 38–43.

———. 2003. *The Green Belt Movement: Sharing the Approach and the Experience*. New York: Lantern Books.

———. 2004a. "A Talk with Nobel Prize Winner Dr. Wangari Maathai." By Tony Cox. NPR News. December 22, 2004. https://www.npr.org/templates/story/story.php?storyId=4240527.

———. 2004b. "The Challenge of AIDS in Africa." Green Belt Movement. December 12, 2004. https://www.greenbeltmovement.org/wangari-maathai/key-speeches-and-articles/challenge-of-AIDS.

———. 2004c. "Wangari Maathai: Nobel Lecture." Lecture, Oslo, December 10, 2004.

———. 2005a. "An Interview with Nobel Peace Prize Winner Wangari Maathai." By Grist Staff. *Grist*, February 16, 2005.

———. 2005b. "Inaugural World Food Law Distinguished Lecture." Lecture, World Food Law Lunch, Howard University, Washington, DC, May 10, 2005.

———. 2005c. "Interview with Wangari Maathai." By Pal Amitabh. *The Progressive*, May 1, 2005.

———. 2005d. "Rise Up and Walk! The Third Annual Nelson Mandela Lecture." Lecture, Johannesburg, July 19, 2005.

———. 2006. "Planting the Future." By Krista Tippett. *On Being*. American Public Media.

———. 2007a. *Unbowed: A Memoir*. New York: Alfred A. Knopf.

———. 2007b. "Unbowed: A Memoir." C-SPAN. September 24, 2007. https://www.c-span.org/video/?201590-1/unbowed-memoir.

―――. 2009a. "After Words with Wangari Maathai." By Nicole Lee. *After Words.* C-Span. April 13, 2009.

―――. 2009b. *The Challenge for Africa.* New York: Pantheon Books.

―――. 2009c. "Interview with the 2004 Nobel Peace Prize Laureate, Wangari Maathai." By Marika Griehsel. Nobel Media AB 2014. April 2, 2009. http://www.nobelprize.org/mediaplayer/index.php?id=1120.

―――. 2009d. "Interview with Wangari Maathai, Environmental Activist and Nobel Laureate." By Marianne Schnall. *Huffington Post,* August 21, 2009. https://www.huffingtonpost.com/marianne-schnall/interview-with -wangari-ma_b_239157.html.

―――. 2010a. *Replenishing the Earth: Spiritual Values for Healing Ourselves and the World.* New York: Doubleday.

―――. 2010b. "I Will Be a Hummingbird—Wangari Maathai (English)." Film by Bill Benenson and Gene Rosow. YouTube. May 11, 2010. https:// youtu.be/IGMW6YWjMxw.

―――. 2011a. "An African Future: Beyond the Culture of Dependency." Open Democracy. Last modified September 27, 2011. https://www .opendemocracy.net/article/an-african-future-beyond-the-culture-of -dependency.

―――. 2011b. "Challenge for Africa." *Sustainability Science* 6 (1): 1–2.

MAS (Municipal Art Society). n.d. Wangari Maathai Award. Municipal Art Society of New York. https://www.mas.org/programs/awards /wangari-maathai-award/.

Materu, Sosteness Francis. 2014. *The Post-Election Violence in Kenya: Domestic and International Legal Responses.* The Hague: Asser Press.

Mazur, Laura, and Louella Miles. 2009. *Conversations with Green Gurus: The Collective Wisdom of Environmental Movers and Shakers.* West Sussex: John Wiley.

Mbaria, John. 2004. "Kenya: East Africa Hails Wangari Maathai's Peace Prize." *East African,* October 11, 2004.

Mbure, Wanjiru G. 2018. "Heroic Transverser: A Rhetorical Analysis of Representations of Wangari Maathai in Kenyan Press." In Mutua, González, and Wolbert, *Rhetorical Legacy of Wangari Maathai,* 63–82.

Michaelson, Marc. 1994. "Wangari Maathai and Kenya's Green Belt Movement: Exploring the Evolution and Potentialities of Consensus Movement Mobilization." *Social Problems* 41 (4): 540–61.

Miller, Norman, and Rodger Yeager. 2018. *Kenya: The Quest for Prosperity.* 3rd ed. New York: Routledge.

Mougoué, Jacqueline-Bethel. 2016. "African Women Do Not Look Good in Wigs: Gender, Beauty Rituals and Cultural Identity in Anglophone Cameroon, 1961–1972." *Feminist Africa* 21:7–22.

Mugo, Micere Githae. 2011. *Writing and Speaking from the Heart of My Mind: Selected Essays and Speeches.* Trenton, NJ: Africa World Press.

Muhonja, Besi Brillian. 2015. "Teaching Moments and Negotiating Motherhood." *JENdA: A Journal of Culture and African Women Studies* 0 (23): 33–52.

————. 2016. "Gender, Archiving, and Recognition: Naming and Erasing in Nairobi's Cityscape." In *Kenya after Fifty: Reconfiguring Education, Gender, and Policy*, edited by Michael Kithinji, Mickie Mwanzia Koster, and Jerono P. Rotich, 171–95. New York: Palgrave Macmillan.

Muigai, Githu. 1993. "Kenya's Opposition and the Crisis of Governance." *African Issues* 21 (1/2): 26–34.

Murunga, Godwin R., and Shadrack W. Nasong'o, eds. 2007. *Kenya: The Struggle for Democracy*. New York: Zed Books.

Mutongi, Kenda. 1999. "'Worries of the Heart': Widowed Mothers, Daughters and Masculinities in Maragoli, Western Kenya, 1940–60." *Journal of African History* 40 (1): 67–86.

Mutua, Eddah, Albert Gonzáalez, and Anke Wolbert, eds. 2018. *The Rhetorical Legacy of Wangari Maathai: Planting the Future*. Lanham, MD: Rowman & Littlefield.

Mutua, Eddah, and Kikuko Omori. 2018. "A Cross-Cultural Approach to Environmental and Peace Work: Wangari Maathai's Use of Mottainai in Kenya." *Journal of Social Encounters* 2 (1): 22–36.

Mutua, Makau. 2008. *Kenya's Quest for Democracy: Taming Leviathan*. Boulder, CO: Lynne Rienner.

Nagel, Mechthild. 2005. "Environmental Justice and Women's Rights: A Tribute to Wangari Maathai." *Wagadu* 2 (1): 1–9.

Namulundah, Florence. 2014. *Wangari Maathai: Visionary, Environmental Leader, Political Activist*. New York: Lantern Books.

Napoli, Donna Jo. 2010. *Mama Miti: Wangari Maathai and the Trees of Kenya*. Illustrated by Aurélia Fronty. New York: Simon & Schuster.

Nchimbi, Rehema J. 2005. "Women's Beauty in the History of Tanzania." PhD diss., University of Cape Town, 2005.

Nerienberg, Danielle, and Mia MacDonald. 2010. "Don't Get Mad, Get Elected! A Conversation with Activist Wangari Maathai." In *Women Writing Resistance*, edited by Browdy de Hernandez, Jennifer, Pauline Dongala, Omotayo Jolaosho, and Anne Serafin, 259–64. Madison: University of Wisconsin Press.

Ngesa, Mildred. 2013. *Kenya: Voting for Our Own: The Dynamics of Tribal Politics in the East African State*. Berlin: Rosa-Luxemburg-Stiftung. http://edoc.vifapol.de/opus/volltexte/2014/5310/pdf/PolicyPaper_07_2013.pdf.

Nivola, Claire. 2008. *Planting the Trees of Kenya: The Story of Wangari Maathai*. New York: Farrar, Straus and Giroux.

Nobel Women's Initiative. N.d. https://nobelwomensinitiative.org.

Norwegian Nobel Committee. 2004. "The Nobel Peace Prize for 2004 to Wangari Maathai." Press release. October 8, 2004. Nobel Prize.

Nyangena, Kenneth O. 2003. "Jomo Kenyatta: An Epitome of Indigenous Pan-Africanism, Nationalism, and Intellectual Production in Kenya." *African Journal of International Affairs* 6 (1/2): 1–18.

Nzegwu, Nkiru. 2004. "Cultural Epistemologies of Motherhood." *JENdA: A Journal of Culture and African Women Studies* 0 (5): n.p.

——. 2006. *Family Matters: Feminist Concepts in African Philosophy of Culture.* Albany: SUNY Press.

——. 2009. "The Epistemological Challenge of Motherhood to Patriliny." *JENdA: A Journal of Culture and African Women Studies* 0 (5): n.p.

Onyango, Leah, Brent Swallow, and Ruth Meinzen-Dick. 2005. "Hydronomics and Terranomics in the Nyando Basin of Western Kenya." Presentation, International Workshop on Africa Water Laws: Plural Legislative Frameworks for Rural Water Management in Africa, Gauteng, South Africa, January 26, 2005.

Oyewumi, Oyeronke. 1997. *The Invention of Women: Making an African Sense of Western Gender Discourses.* Minneapolis: University of Minnesota Press.

——. 2003. "Abiyamo: Theorizing African Motherhood." *Jenda: A Journal of Culture and African Women Studies* 4 (1): 1–7.

——. 2015. *What Gender Is Motherhood?: Changing Yoru`ba' Ideals of Power, Procreation, and Identity in the Age of Modernity.* New York: Palgrave Macmillan.

Pala, Achola O. 2013. "Dimensions of African Motherhood." *JENdA: A Journal of Culture and African Women Studies* 23: 8–10.

Plant-for-the-Planet. n.d. https://www.plant-for-the-planet.org/en/home. Accessed March 2018.

Presbey, Gail M. 2013. "Women's Empowerment: The Insights of Wangari Maathai." *Journal of Global Ethics* 9 (3): 277–92.

Prevot, Franck. 2015. *Wangari Maathai: The Woman Who Planted a Million Trees.* Watertown, MA: Charlesbridge.

Sears, Priscilla. 1991. "Wangari Maathai: 'You Strike the Woman . . . .'" *Context: A Quarterly of Human Sustainable Culture* 28: 55–57.

Speich, Daniel. 2009. "The Kenyan Style of 'African Socialism': Developmental Knowledge Claims and the Explanatory Limits of the Cold War." *Diplomatic History* 33 (3): 449–66.

Sudarkasa, Niara. 2004. "Conceptions of Motherhood in Nuclear and Extended Families, with Special Reference to Comparative Studies Involving African Societies." *JENdA: A Journal of Culture and African Women Studies* 0 (5): n.p.

Taking Root: The Vision of Wangari Maathai. 2008. DVD. Directed by Lisa Merton and Alan Dater. Marlboro, NJ: Marlboro Productions.

Tutu, Desmond. 2007. *Desmond Tutu on Ubuntu.* YouTube. https://www.youtube.com/watch?v=ftjdDOfTzbk.

——. 2012. *Ubuntu: A Brief Description.* YouTube. https://www.youtube.com/watch?v=wg49mvZ2V5U.

——. n.d. *Who We Are: Human Uniqueness and the African Spirit of Ubuntu; Desmond Tutu, Templeton Prize 2013.* YouTube. https://www.youtube.com/watch?v=0wZtfqZ271w.

UNESCO. 2015. *Women in African History: Wangari Maathai.* London: HarperCollins UK.

United Nations. Sustainable Development Knowledge Platform. https://sustainabledevelopment.un.org/?menu=1300.

University of Pittsburgh. 2013. "Wangari Maathai Trees and Garden to Be Dedicated." Press release. University of Pittsburgh News Services. September 18, 2013. http://www.news.pitt.edu/news/wangari-maathai -trees-and-garden-be-dedicated.

wa Tushabe, Tushabe. 2013. "Memoirs of Motherhood: Reflections on Pedagogical Motherhood in Community." *JENdA: A Journal of Culture and African Women Studies* 0 (23): 11–31.

Wagner, Casey L. 2016. "Restoring Relationship: How the Methodologies of Wangari Maathai and the Green Belt Movement in Post-Colonial Kenya Achieve Environmental Healing and Women's Empowerment." MA thesis, East Tennessee State University. http://dc.etsu.edu/etd/3164.

Wambui, Betty. 2018. "Buffeted: Developing an Afro Feminist Response to Environmental Questions." In *African Philosophy and the Epistemic Marginalization of Women,* edited by Jonathan O. Chimakonam and Louise du Toit, 167–88. New York: Routledge.

Wangari Gardens. n.d. https://wangarigardens.wordpress.com.

"Wangari Maathai Arrested." 1991. *Race, Poverty and the Environment* 2 (3/4): 9.

Wangari Maathai Foundation. n.d. Wangari Muta Maathai House. http://wangarimaathai.org/wangari-house/. Accessed February 2018.

Winter, Jeanette. 2008. *Wangari's Trees of Peace: A True Story from Africa.* Boston: Houghton Mifflin Harcourt.

WMI (Wangari Maathai Institute for Peace and Environmental Studies). 2010. *Strategic Plan 2010–2020.* Nairobi: University of Nairobi.

———. n.d. "WMI Project Architectural and Land Use Plan Brief." Wangari Maathai Institute for Peace and Environmental Studies. University of Nairobi. https://wmi.uonbi.ac.ke/node/4030.

Index